The Economics of the Colour Bar

*A study of the economic origins and
consequences of racial segregation
in South Africa*

W. H. HUTT

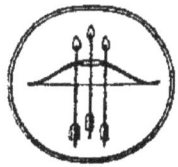

Published for
THE INSTITUTE OF ECONOMIC AFFAIRS
by
ANDRE DEUTSCH

Large Print Edition published 2014 by Skyler J. Collins.
Visit: www.skylerjcollins.com

First published by the Institute of Economic Affairs, London in 1964.

ISBN-13: 978-1495395703
ISBN-10: 1495395707

CONTENTS

		Page
	Prefatory Note	4
	Foreword	5
	The Author	6

Chapter

1	The Problem and its Setting	9
2	The South African Background	14
3	Colour Prejudice and Colour Resentment	23
4	The Poor Whites	32
5	Injustices to Afrikaners	38
	Appendix—'Chinese Slavery'	45
6	Africans in the Mines	47
7	The First Colour Bar Act	58
	Appendix—'Collective Bargaining and the non-Whites'	66
8	The 'Civilised Labour' Era	68
9	Racial Integration and Industrial Growth	82
10	Africans in the Towns	87
11	Africans and Labour Unions	101
12	The Group Areas Policy	110
13	Job Reservation	117
14	The Indians	121
15	The Direction of African Labour	126
16	The Border Areas	139
17	The Bantustans	151
18	The Market is Colour-Blind	173
	Statistical Appendix	181
	Bibliography	183
	Index	185

PREFATORY NOTE

Professor W. H. Hutt has written this book as an economist. His central discussion is of economic causes and consequences and he touches only marginally on other aspects, political, sociological, philosophical.

Readers may differ from some of the judgments on non-economic aspects of the subject, but the Institute considers that Professor Hutt's effort to explain *apartheid* makes a new contribution to the debate that has been overlooked both by supporters and opponents. It does not necessarily accept his argument or conclusions, but believes he has written an informed, stimulating and controversial history and analysis of *apartheid* that can do nothing but good if it provokes discussion and re-appraisal of uncritical attitudes on all sides.

The central theme is that if the English in South Africa had continued the development of a liberal economy, it would have prevented or ameliorated the racial tensions that have been exacerbated by the restrictionist policies arising from the Nationalist Government's racialist doctrines and the efforts of the higher-paid white workers to protect privileged positions in the labour market.

Although Professor Hutt writes dispassionately as an academic, there is ample evidence in his record of public protest of his moral revulsion against the injustices to the non-white peoples of South Africa.

November, 1963.   I.E.A.

FOREWORD

THE argument of this essay is illustrated mainly by reference to policies and conditions in the Republic (formerly the Union) of South Africa. Through the pressure of world opinion and the force of internal criticism, these policies and conditions are currently in process of significant modification – some changes being in a seemingly liberal direction and others in a seemingly totalitarian direction. The changes have been continuing whilst this book has been in the press; but its purpose is not to provide an up-to-date account of the racial situation in South Africa. It simply uses the experience of that country in an attempt to expose the ultimate origins of colour injustices generally. Similar origins can, I suggest, be discerned for all colour, racial, caste, class or similar injustices wherever they may exist.

March 1964 W. H. HUTT

THE AUTHOR

WILLIAM HAROLD HUTT was born in 1899. He was educated in London and served in the R.F.C. and R.A.F. from 1917 to 1919. After the war he studied at the London School of Economics. He worked for several years with Benn Brothers, London, and joined the University of Cape Town in 1928. He was appointed Professor of Commerce and Dean of the Faculty of Commerce in 1931 and has held this post ever since.

He has written several works on theoretical and applied economics. His books include *The Theory of Collective Bargaining*, 1930; *Economists and the Public*, 1936; *The Theory of Idle Resources*, 1939; *Plan for Reconstruction*, 1943; *Keynesianism—Retrospect and Prospect*, 1963. He has also written numerous articles in economic journals, including several dealing with economic aspects of South African colour problems.

Professor Hutt has long been a critic of racial policies in South Africa. His fears were aroused before the election in 1948 of the Afrikaner Nationalist Government. Through the Statute of Westminster (1931) the British Government had relinquished effective control over the constitutional development of South Africa. The 1934 South African Status Act took a further step in this direction and in 1937 Professor Hutt tried to arouse South African public opinion to the danger that the entrenched clauses in the constitution, which safeguarded *inter alia* the right of coloured men in the Cape to vote on the common roll, were being undermind. He warned his adopted country through the columns of the *Cape Times* that it had carelessly torn up its constitution. For this he was rebuked by the paper for irresponsibility. Since 1948 Professor Hutt has consistently opposed the South African Government's policy of *apartheid*.

In 1955 his passport was withdrawn by the Department of the Interior but returned after the matter had been raised in Parliament. In 1961, as South Africa was seceding from the Commonwealth, he argued in *The Times* that all South African citizens, irrespective of race, colour or creed should be offered British citizenship.

'It is a striking historical fact that the development of capitalism has been accompanied by a major reduction in the extent to which particular religious, racial, or social groups have operated under special handicaps in respect of their economic activities; have, as the saying goes, been discriminated against. The substitution of contract arrangements for status arrangements was the first step toward the freeing of the serfs in the Middle Ages. The preservation of Jews through the Middle Ages was possible because of the existence of a market sector in which they could operate and maintain themselves despite official persecution. Puritans and Quakers were able to migrate to the New World because they could accumulate the funds to do so in the market despite disabilities imposed on them in other aspects of their life. The Southern states after the Civil War took many measures to impose legal restrictions on Negroes. One measure which was never taken on any scale was the establishment of barriers to the ownership of either real or personal property. The failure to impose such barriers clearly did not reflect any special concern to avoid restrictions on Negroes. It reflected rather, a basic belief in private property which was so strong that it overrode the desire to discriminate against Negroes. The maintenance of the general rules of private property and of capitalism have been a major source of opportunity for Negroes and have permitted them to make greater progress than they otherwise could have made. To take a more general example, the preserves of discrimination in any society are the areas that are most monopolistic in character, whereas discrimination against groups of particular colour or religion is least in those areas where there is the greatest freedom of competition.'

MILTON FRIEDMAN, *Capitalism and Freedom*

CHAPTER I

THE PROBLEM AND ITS SETTING

WHY DO the non-white peoples of the world today enjoy a much lower average standard of material well-being than the white peoples? The answer is compounded of history, climate, custom, powerful inertias, insecurity for investment, and legislative barriers to employment. How far can their inferior economic status be said to be caused by natural handicaps and how far by injustice at the hands of white people? Usually there is a mixture of causes.

For instance, the failure to have stamped out disease, which still retards the development of many tropical regions, is due partly to inertia in the effective spread of medical knowledge, partly to tribal superstitions and customs, partly to climatic factors. Is there an element of injustice here?

Similarly, investment insecurity is partly a question of history and partly a matter of the slowness with which an understanding of the vital role of property – and its prerequisites – has spread to primitive communities. Some backward peoples and their advisers have ignored, or have failed to create, the conditions necessary for an inward flow of fructifying capital to provide productive equipment and foster the inborn powers of the people. Consequently, where capital flowed freely and rapidly from Western Europe to the under-developed regions of North America before 1914, it now tends to avoid areas like India and Africa, despite their enormous development potential. Is that situation due to injustice?

ECONOMIC 'INJUSTICE'
As an economist, I shall attribute 'injustice' to any policy or action which is intended to perpetuate the inferiority of material standards or status of any racial group. The inheritance of inferior circumstances or status cannot usefully

be regarded as 'unjust', except to the extent to which developed countries or colonising powers can be shown to be deliberately withholding opportunities from the underdeveloped areas or colonised peoples.

Nevertheless we must ourselves be just in evaluating the past. Although we may deplore the era of slavery, we must remember that the enslavement of primitive peoples was not condemned by the religious and ethical codes which existed in the era in which it flourished. John Wesley was not unjust to the children of his day when he laid it down that they should be allowed neither to talk nor smile at Sunday school! The gradual evolution of ideas about what is appropriate in the relations of one man to another, one caste or race to another has, significantly, been fostered by economic progress more than by any other cause.

Some injustices may be due more to class barriers than to colour barriers. For instance, there is much resentment felt against Portugal as an intransigent colonial power. But no legally enacted colour bars exist in any Portuguese territory; and a South African who crosses into Mozambique is at once struck by the wholly different attitude, at least superficially, towards colour. Yet the overwhelming majority of the Africans of Mozambique are extremely poor. Some critics conclude that Portugal maintains a *de facto* if not a legal colour bar. But there are approximately an equal number of Whites and non-Whites with 'assimilado' status (that is, who have achieved both literacy and the ability to live at defined civilised standards) who have long enjoyed absolute equality of rights before the law.[1] Yet only 160,000 out of the population of 6.6 million enjoy this status and only 5 per cent of the non-white assimilados are Africans (the rest are Indians and half-castes). If the evident backwardness of the masses is caused by deliberate policy rather than by unrestrained population growth and a paucity of natural resources, there is certainly cause for complaints of class injustice, but not of colour injustice. But educated and responsible non-Whites are not subjected, in the Portuguese

---

[1] The system has recently been changed. Any African may now choose whether he wishes to be subject to tribal or Portuguese law. If he chooses the latter, he has the right to vote (whatever that means in a dictatorship) but he then becomes liable to taxation.

territories, to the indignities and humiliations they suffer in South Africa.[1]

THE MERITS AND DEFECTS OF COLONIALISM
The current, almost world-wide disapproval of colonialism is derived from the idea that the colonising nations have held or are holding the colonised peoples in some sort of subjection. Nearly all of us talk of the African races having recently obtained their 'freedom'. Yet in most of the Western-held colonies, the rule of law has been long established; the highest standards of integrity in administration have been maintained; and where colonial administrations have sought to preserve tribal customs, institutions or forms of government, and so followed policies that tended to some extent to preserve the relative backwardness of the indigenous peoples, repression was certainly never the purpose. The spirit of that policy was essentially one of tolerance, even respect, for different ways of living; it was an attitude that facilitated the task of harmonious and just administration; and for this reason the colonising powers did not actively discourage primitive customs or supersede systems of authority incompatible with the emergence of modern communities.

It may be charged further that insufficient was done to educate the natives as administrators and for eventual self-government. Whatever the shortcomings, the motive was not reactionary. Colonial officials, it is true, sometimes came to regard themselves as a kind of ruling aristocracy, and no doubt regarded 'educated natives' as a disturbing element. And white settlers came quite naturally to believe in their innate superiority, moral and mental, over non-Whites who were assumed to be destined to play a subordinate role. The factor of 'prejudice' seems to have arisen in this manner. But prejudice is simply a manifestation of powerful custom. I shall suggest that it will dissolve under the pressures released by economic liberalism as rapidly as other customs that are inappropriate in a wealthier and more diversified economy.

In this book I am concerned with influences that are hindering the dissolution of prejudice and anachronistic

---

[1]Inter-marriage is a crime in South Africa. It is officially encouraged in Mozambique.

custom, that is, with factors that may be held to be responsible for the 'injustice' presently endured by some – if not most – of the non-white peoples of the world.

I shall illustrate my thesis almost entirely by reference to experience in the Republic of South Africa where I have been living whilst my ideas were forming. But the lessons learned from a study of colour bars, *apartheid* and other manifestations of colour prejudice in South Africa, are of direct relevance wherever skin pigmentation or other racial characteristics serve as a principle for confining individuals to any sort of economic or social inferiority.[1]

Without attempting a comprehensive account of colour relations – economic, social or political – in South Africa,[2] I shall try to identify (a) the forces that have tended to dissolve the economic and social inferiority of the non-white classes, and (b) the opposing forces – constituting the injustice – that have tended, deliberately or otherwise, to perpetuate this inferiority. In the final Chapter I shall sum up what I hope the reader himself will have gathered from the facts and interpretations presented about the nature of these forces.

Now my interpretations of the facts will amount to a criticism of the thinking – not the sincerity – of many of the more vociferous of those who campaign, with tenacity and courage, against colour injustices. I shall, on the whole, be questioning the insight and wisdom of people with no axe to grind – the vastly more numerous disinterested opponents of racial discrimination.[3] It is ideas and stereotypes, not aims and purposes, which I shall be challenging.

Among my tasks will be that of dealing with the opinions of those who stoutly and honestly defend colour bars, the supremacy of Whites, 'baasskap', *apartheid*, 'separate development', and so forth. In this part of my task I do not

---

[1] The present government of the Republic of South Africa deny that this is the purpose of *apartheid* (separate development). I propose, however, to show why that must be the consequence of their policy.
[2] See Bibliography, p. 183.
[3] There are of course politicians who seek to exacerbate colour resentments solely because they think it will help them in their manœuvring for power. I am not writing for them. They and their henchmen will misrepresent and reject my thesis because it may hamper the achievement of their ambitions.

feel I am likely to be seriously misunderstood. But when I expose the frequently inadequate knowledge and defective reasoning of burningly sincere do-gooders, anxious to exterminate all vestiges of colour privilege or subordinacy, I run the risk of being suspected of hostility to ideals which I share. May I assure hasty critics that I deplore colour discrimination no less than they do; the difference is that I believe it can be eradicated without bloodshed or the worse injustices that would accompany their methods.

CHAPTER 2

THE SOUTH AFRICAN BACKGROUND

THE racial composition of the population of the Republic of South Africa may be summarised briefly. The Whites (inappropriately termed 'Europeans') make up about one-fifth. The home language of about 60 per cent – the Afrikaners – is Afrikaans, and of the remainder, English. History has created and the politicians have perpetuated a political, and to some extent an economic, cleavage between the two white sections. Africans (formerly called 'Natives' but now officially, although rather inappropriately, termed 'Bantu'[1]) form about two-thirds of the population; the Coloureds, a race of half-castes, about one-tenth of the total; and Asiatics, mainly Indians, about 2 to 3 per cent.

THE ORIGIN OF RACE CONFLICT

To understand the relations between these groups, it is essential to grasp the remarkable complexity of the colour situation; but any attempt adequately to explain the origins of that complexity would involve a long excursion into history. It is possible in this Chapter only to sketch the background.

In 1652, Jan van Riebeeck established a white settlement in Cape Town for the Dutch East India Company, to serve as a half-way house to the Dutch East Indies. The company had no intention of establishing a colony in Africa. It merely wanted an assured supply of water, vegetables, fruit and wine to preserve the health of their crews sailing to or from its East Indian possessions. Nevertheless, its employees spread into the interior of the Cape and by the end of the eighteenth century a virtual colony had emerged. But partly because of the company's reluctance to colonise, and partly because the aboriginal Hottentots and Bushmen did not

---

[1]The present government wishes to avoid the word 'African'.

make good servants, it imported slaves to the settlement, mainly from Malaya. At that period, the aversion to intermarriage was much less strong than it became later. Almost from the foundation of the Cape settlement, there was interbreeding between White and non-White. As a result (together with a later inter-mixture of African blood) there emerged the race of half-castes known today as the Coloured people. It constitutes the most unjustly treated, the most cheerful and the most lovable group of people I have ever known.

The British occupation, which dates from 1806, differed from the Dutch in that colonisation was, in a sense, its purpose, more obviously so after the arrival of the 1820 settlers. The existing white community, mainly of Dutch origin (with more numerous subordinate classes of Hottentots, Coloureds and Malays, free or enslaved) was taken over by Britain. This white community, usually known as 'Boers' at the end of the last and the beginning of the present century, tended to regard itself as subject to 'imperial domination', until the declaration of republican status in 1961. Yet the new regime was relatively liberal ('liberal' in the old sense[1]); no attempt was made to suppress Dutch institutions;[2] the use of the Dutch language was permitted, and it survived in the form of Afrikaans (which, together with English, is today one of the official languages of the Republic); and Roman Dutch Law remains the law of South Africa. Moreover, in their relations with non-Whites the British authorities developed a policy which has often been described as humanitarian. Slavery was abolished in 1834.

---

[1]That is, what the Americans are now calling 'libertarian'. I propose in this essay to follow the example of Professor Milton Friedman of the University of Chicago, using the term 'liberal' in its original connotation, and avoiding the term 'libertarian'.

[2]For instance, in spite of the British Municipal Corporations Act of 1835, the administrative system of 'Landdrosts and Heemraden' (as distinct from Mayors, Aldermen and Councillors), which had been inaugurated under the Dutch East India Company, persisted until late in the century and influenced the whole pattern of administration and justice in South Africa. Liberal influences from Europe seem, in fact, to have been introduced a few years before the British occupation, during the brief regime under which the Cape was subject to rule by the Dutch (from 1803 to 1806), largely through the enlightenment of the Governor of the Cape, de Mist.

THE GROWTH OF AFRIKANERDOM

The spirit of tolerance in British policy had the defects of its virtues. Whereas the Dutch East India Company had suppressed the French language of the Huguenot settlers who had arrived in 1688, forcing the submergence of their culture into the Dutch, the survival in the Cape of the Dutch language and the traditions of the Dutch colonists permitted a separate white community to persist, with its own language, church and sociological background. This development profoundly influenced subsequent history. For the 'Dutch' section – the Boers or Afrikaners – came to feel that they were in danger of losing their identity. They thought their culture, ideals and way of life were threatened by the more aggressive and more self-confident traditions (backed by habits of industry, thrift, commercial knowledge and capital) of the British. Yet influences which tended to spread the advantages enjoyed by the British immigrants were normally represented as 'Anglicisation'. Moreover, many of the Boers were inclined to think of the enforcement of a régime in the Cape which failed to entrench white privilege and recognise the reality of an inherent white superiority as 'imperial domination'. In the pages which follow we shall see how the gradual emancipation of the Boer nation (the Afrikaners) from the bonds of 'British imperialism' was followed by an equally gradual introduction, by those liberated, of laws and administration which sought to subject the non-Whites to permanent inferiority of status and condition.

After the 1830s, it is inappropriate to refer to the 'Dutch' community of South Africa, although they continued to be known as that until this century. Except through their religion, they had little in common with the people of their original homeland, and their language, having become almost entirely spoken and not written, was rapidly simplified to what is now recognised to be a separate language, Afrikaans. I shall henceforth refer to this section of the white people as 'the Afrikaners'.

THE VOORTREKKERS
The most serious cause of the schism among the Whites was the indignation of the Afrikaners at the mildest official ten-

dencies towards liberalism in respect of colour. The ideal of equality of treatment for all in a multi-racial society was anathema to a group which had become used to slave-owning; and, following the freeing of the slaves in 1834, many of the Afrikaner families fled into the interior, thus initiating, in 1836, what has become known as the Great Trek. The advancing 'Voortrekkers', as the colonising Afrikaners are called, occupied a more or less empty interior, at first obtaining the areas they settled by treaty rather than by force of arms. But in the course of the Trek, they eventually came into violent conflict with African tribes, and because the Voortrekkers were victorious in the wars, the Africans were eventually driven into demarcated areas known as 'reserves', which have survived until today.[1]

Moving deeply into the interior, the Voortrekkers formed two new large, independent republics known as the Orange Free State and the Transvaal. These republics adopted democratic constitutions except for the provision that there should be no equality in church or state between Black and White, a principle that perpetuated attitudes of mind and conviction with which policy-makers still have to contend to this day. The trekking Afrikaners had also moved into Natal, but that area fell under British control very soon afterwards (in 1843) and the emigration of colonists from Britain eventually caused it to become the most homogeneous English-speaking part of South Africa.

During the British régime in Natal, large numbers of Indians were brought to South Africa. Very shortly after settlement had begun, sugar showed prospects of becoming a vital product in the economy. But much labour was required, and at first attempts were made to persuade the local Africans to undertake the job. For various reasons they did not succeed, and it was then decided to arrange for indentured labour to be brought from India for work on the plantations. Indian immigration began in 1859 and was finally ended in 1911. In the meantime, traders from India had followed the indentured workers and a settled Indian community (some of whom moved out of Natal to better opportunities in other parts of South Africa) had come into being.

---

[1]The British settlers in the Eastern Province experienced similar conflicts.

UNION AND DISUNITY

At the end of the century, the Boer War, with the rights and wrongs of which we are not concerned, brought the Orange Free State and the Transvaal under British sovereignty. At the settlement in 1902, the victors granted self-government to the vanquished, subject to the safeguarding of political rights for non-Afrikaners, which the war had ostensibly been fought to bring about. In 1910, all four colonies, the Cape, Natal, the Orange Free State and the Transvaal, were merged into the Union of South Africa.

Under the Act of Union, political independence was conferred upon the four colonies, which were joined under a unitary constitution; but non-white franchise and language rights were reserved by the British Crown. The British connection remained important henceforth for two main reasons only: first, sentiment, which had made the transfer of power acceptable to the British electorate; and second, because of the attempt to entrench constitutionally (a) the political rights of the non-Whites – which had traditionally existed only in one part of the new Union, the Cape, and (b) equal rights for English and Dutch (later Afrikaans) as 'official languages'. Nevertheless, the Afrikaners' fight against 'British imperialism' continued and was inspired by the generation and maintenance of an atmosphere of dogged resistance against forces which were held to be threatening 'die Boerenasie' (the Boer nation). The Nationalist Party achieved power and have sought to maintain themselves permanently in power by indoctrination through education, by exploitation of nationalist emotions and by the maintenance of a continuous atmosphere of emergency and struggle against 'external enemies'.[1]

Of the four colonies merged, it was in the Cape alone that the non-Whites had any sort of effective political rights;[2] and in order to get the consent of the Cape for unification it had been essential that there should appear to be no risk of these rights being removed. Moreover, the entrenched clauses (which were believed to eliminate the risk) were probably an equally necessary condition for the acceptance of

---
[1] See Chapter 5, p. 42.
[2] In Natal there was some possibility of non-Whites qualifying for the franchise but only a handful did, in fact, qualify.

the South Africa Act (which constituted the South African Act of Union) by the British Parliament. Indeed, in the debate on the Act British statesmen confidently expressed the view that the 'liberalism' of the Cape would gradually spread to the other provinces. But the march of time belied this faith and proved the entrenchments to be quite ineffective.

In 1931, mainly in the hope of appeasing Afrikaner Nationalism, the British passed the Statute of Westminster which quietly removed (although this was not clear at the time) the authority of the British Crown to veto any dishonouring of the entrenched clauses. The Status Act, passed by the South African Parliament in 1934, took a further step in this direction. What confused the leaders of the coloured people and their friends at this time was that the provision requiring a two-thirds majority of both Houses of Parliament to amend the entrenched clauses remained in the constitution. Moreover, even the Nationalist leaders gave the most solemn assurances that they would regard the entrenchments as binding. Indeed, they expressed deep resentment at those who ventured to suggest that the clauses in question might not, in fact, be honoured. The Speaker of the House of Assembly went so far as to assure the Africans (who, through a resolution of the Transkeian General Council, had expressed grave concern at the move) that the entrenchments had been strengthened. Public opinion was temporarily reassured. Gradually, however, the implications of the change began to sink home and grave perturbation developed.

But the South African government in the middle and late 1930s was an unholy and uneasy coalition, and if the liberal-minded members of the coalition had raised the issue it would have threatened cabinet unity. Indeed, when I myself tried to arouse public opinion in 1937 by referring to the manner in which the public had been misled, I was strongly attacked by the *Cape Times* (in a controversy which went into several issues[1]) for irresponsibility.[2] I had charged

---

[1] *Cape Times*, 20 August, 1937. The exchange ceased on 31 August, 1937.
[2] In fairness I should add that, since the fall of the coalition and the outbreak of the war, the *Cape Times* has been the most influential outlet in South Africa for the consistent and persistent expression of enlightened opinion.

that we had carelessly 'torn up our Constitution'. But no steps to rectify the position were taken, or even seriously considered.

DEMOCRACY DISHONOURED

When the Afrikaner Nationalists eventually obtained the upper hand, in 1948, they immediately took steps to prove that the Constitution had been torn up. By various manœuvres, which included an attack on the judiciary, an attempt to transform Parliament into a High Court, and finally packing the Senate with their own representatives, they secured the two-thirds majority needed for the abolition of the existing non-white voting rights. Far from the 'liberalism' of the Cape having spread to the rest of South Africa, as the British Parliament had been led to expect before Union, the Transvaal and the Orange Free State traditions of 'no equality in church or state' had been forced on the whole community, and the Coloureds had been deprived of a political status they had held for a century.[1] Of course, political representation of a minority is no guarantee of economic justice for that minority. The Minister of Coloured Affairs argued recently in defence of the abolition of the political rights which the coloured people had enjoyed, that these rights had left 80 per cent of them 'backward and poor, with leaders deserting them and trying to gain admission to the white masses'.[2] But their removal from the common roll has been felt as a humiliating deprivation of status.

Now although the absence of political rights does not necessarily mean the loss of freedom, it does imply that one factor is missing which, together with others, may guarantee freedom. Groups with no voting rights may well be subject to the rule of law and enjoy full equality before law. This is in fact the position of foreigners in most democratic countries. It would be absurd to suggest that, when we decide to live in foreign, democratic countries, where we have no voting rights, we are less free than we are at home. Similarly,

---

[1] They have since been represented in Parliament, not on a common roll, but by four white members. Indians now have no representation. But Coloured and Indians together exceed the Afrikaners in number.
[2] *Cape Times*, 13 May, 1963.

it would be absurd to suggest that Swiss women, who do not enjoy the franchise, are less free or feel less free than their husbands or brothers. But I am not defending the revocation of the entrenched clauses. On the contrary, I believe that that step, breaking as it has done respect for constitutional entrenchments, may well prove disastrous for the white minority in South Africa, and perhaps in other African States.

We do not easily think of the African, Coloured or Indian subjects of the Republic of South Africa as being subject to colonial rule. But some writers have regarded 'the Native Reserves' of South Africa as colonised areas. This notion is far from satisfactory; for, as we shall see, policy in the Republic has aimed with increasing deliberateness at preventing those forms of development to which the profit motive would direct investment; whereas it has been the essence of the colonialism which has fallen into such disrepute that commercial incentives have been allowed to determine the course of economic advance. The influx of private capital into the 'Native Areas' of South Africa has been controlled with growing stringency, and for several years now it has been brought virtually to an end. Admittedly, white traders and a few hotel keepers, garage proprietors, and others have been permitted in the African territories; many of them have, indeed, made fortunes through the phenomenal growth of the African's purchasing power during the last few decades; but on the whole the acquisition of property by Whites – including the establishment of industries – has been restrained.

The motive of these restraints has in part been that of preserving ownership for the Africans, and it has not been entirely unsuccessful. For instance, if the purchase of land by the Whites had not been forbidden, given the other restrictions on the productivity and hence on the incomes of the Africans, it is likely that a large proportion of the most valuable land would have come to be owned by the Whites. That would not have been an outcome to be deplored from all points of view; for it would almost certainly have meant a large increase in the agricultural productivity of the reserves, an incomparably larger internally-earned income, and hence a much larger permanently resident African population within their homelands. But it would have created one of the chief apparent injustices of colonialism, a minority race acquiring ownership of the bulk of a conspicuous form of capital.

EFFECTS OF THE RESTRICTIONS ON INVESTMENT

If policy had been to encourage the investment of private capital in the reserves, however, the scant natural resources of these areas would have been more rapidly and intensively developed; and again the material benefits would have been largest among the Africans themselves. But the sociological consequences of the rising standards of living – the inevitable weakening of tribal customs and tradition – would not have been welcomed either by the South African Government or by the chiefs. And one of the principal objects of recent policy has been the prevention of any such developments. Thus, in recently granting some measure of local autonomy (so-called 'self-government') to the Transkei, the necessity to protect the Africans from the 'wolves', the white capitalists, has been emphasised by spokesmen for *apartheid*. There is a familiar, contemporary ring about the catch-phrases used to justify a policy which permits only such forms of material progress as the state finds expedient.[1] Yet in curbing the profit incentive to investment (and in causing therefore a slowing down of the material advancement of the Africans), *apartheid* has warded off the emergence of a situation which is, on the whole, regarded as unjust. That is, it has (within the reserves) prevented a minority of Whites or foreign investors from becoming the owners of a large part of the physical resources which provide employment for Blacks.

But are not the wiser social critics those who perceive that the fundamental injustice suffered by the Africans originates in those hindrances to private investment which have condemned them as a whole to avoidable backwardness, ignorance, illiteracy, poverty and high mortality. This is indeed the central theme of the book.

---

[1] See Chapter 17, pp. 158–160.

CHAPTER 3

COLOUR PREJUDICE AND COLOUR RESENTMENT

THE racial problems of the Republic of South Africa are, I believe, incomparably more complex than those of any other country in the world. There is more ethnological and sociological variety; wider dispersion in the standards of education, earning ability and money incomes per head; and the difficulties which arise in any attempt to design an institutional framework under which peaceful relations can be achieved among the members of this conglomeration appear at first almost insuperable. What further complicates the problem is a schism between the English-speaking and the Afrikaans-speaking sections of the white people. It is desirable to deal with this division among the Whites in order to understand the broad relations between Whites and non-Whites.[1]

The feelings of injustice which are so often harboured by white or non-white classes or races do not originate wholly from a feeling that economic opportunities are unfairly withheld by custom, collusive action or legal enactment. If the social segregation of the races survived the general achievement of economic equality (which, in my judgment, it would not), it would still evoke resentments. The longing for improved rank, status, prestige and respect appears to be of greater relative importance. Thus, the break-up of the Rhodesian Federation may be interpreted as evidence that African leaders place a higher value on the dignity of their race than they do upon prospective material advantages (like a falling death rate, improving nutrition and rising real income)[2] or political advantages like freedom of expres-

---

[1] I discuss it in Chapter 4.
[2] But what these leaders have failed to perceive, I think, is that the rise in standards of living and the growth in equality of opportunity which

sion; for those benefits are less likely to survive with the passing of colonial responsibility. Yet as we shall see later on,[1] recent legislation in South Africa seems to have been deliberately aimed at humiliating the non-Whites, particularly in the Immorality Act and the Group Areas Act.

RACE HATRED: PREJUDICE AND RESENTMENT

We can, I think, classify racial hatreds into (a) colour prejudice, i.e., prejudice against and contempt for races of 'inferior' status to ourselves, and (b) colour resentment, i.e., envy of (yet reluctantly admitted respect for) races of superior status to ourselves. After 35 years of observation in South Africa, I should say that there is no colour prejudice on the part of an under-privileged or backward race against a privileged or advanced race, or against those of lighter skin or 'European' type features. Envy, resentment and indignation, yes; hatred, possibly; but 'prejudice', no. Lightly coloured persons take every possible opportunity of passing for white and although there is a big economic advantage for them if they succeed, that is by no means the whole reason for their wishing to do so. The standards of beauty among non-Whites appear to have been subtly moulded by the prestige which attaches to a white skin and white features.[2]

---

the maintenance of the Federation could have promoted, was likely to have engendered (albeit gradually) the respect which they felt had been withheld from them. Their pride and resentments, however natural, may have inspired actions which the rank and file of their people, at any rate, may come to regret.

[1] See Chapter 12.

[2] A well-meaning English lady who had assisted at a nursery school for Coloured children in Cape Town once decided to buy in London a consignment of brown coloured dolls to distribute as Christmas presents to children of more or less the same colour. To her horror, she found that she had blundered. The Coloured children all wanted white dolls!

Many years ago, a quite distinguished, rather lightly coloured headmaster of a secondary school for children of his race, was most embarrassed when he had to accept on his staff a brilliant young schoolmaster whose skin happened to be nearly as black as an African's. Yet this headmaster had been a doughty fighter against colour prejudice. When this perfectly respectable but darkly coloured member of his staff began to get friendly with his nearly white daughter, the headmaster, who in

Liberal-minded white leaders have sometimes said: 'the non-Whites no more wish to mix with us than we wish to mix with them.' That is wishful thinking and wholly wrong. There is no group horror at inter-marriage on the part of Africans, Asiatics and Coloureds comparable to that which exists among the Whites, provided it occurs within the bounds set by their marriage codes and is in the right colour direction. Of course the Africans, living as they do under a régime in which racial inter-mixture is condemned by powerful social convention, tend to inhibit thoughts of it; and the psychological discipline so exerted is strengthened by the ties of tribal custom. Moreover, Africans in the Western Cape tend rather to despise the Coloureds as the inferior group among the privileged and envied classes, an attitude which is reinforced or rationalised by their disapproval (from the standpoint of the sturdy morality of pagan behaviour and its associated dignity) of the addiction of many Coloureds to drink and dagga-smoking and their frequent boisterous conduct. But that is a disapproval of breeding rather than of breed; and the conservative among the Africans regard equally unfavourably their own 'tsotsi', whose behaviour pattern is not so different from that of the Coloured 'skollies'.[1] Some Africans have tried to pass for Coloured or succeeded in so doing, whether mainly for the economic advantages (which are not inconsiderable) or in order to enjoy the higher status it is difficult to tell;

---

other matters had always been a man of principle and courage, felt compelled to forbid the friendship.

Not long ago my wife was invited to act as one of the judges in a beauty contest for African girls in Cape Town. The competitors all wore elegant and fashionable (if cheap) evening gowns. As an artist, my wife was most struck by the dignity and fine bearing of girls with typical African features; but she was warned by her more experienced fellow judges that it would be tactful to accept the standards of the hundreds of Africans who formed the audience, the consensus of whose opinion was expressed in applause as the competitors filed past. Judged by this criterion, there was no doubt that many Africans in the towns have already come to assess the beauty of their girls, in figure and features, in the light of the currently accepted white standards. This phenomenon is strikingly illustrated in the 'pin-up' pictures and advertisements in magazines published expressly for Africans.

[1] The 'tsotsi' among the Africans and the 'skollies' among the Coloureds correspond more or less to the 'leather-jackets' of Britain and America.

others have married Coloured women or live with Coloured concubines. And there are innumerable evidences that the attitude of races towards inter-marriage differs considerably according to whether it is viewed from the side of the poorer or subordinate races or from the side of the wealthier or privileged races.[1] Thus, among the Whites it tends to be regarded with what appears superficially to be a natural repugnance, so insidiously have prestige factors affected moral judgments.[2]

The African intelligentsia have certainly tried to model their manners and demeanour upon that of Whites, particularly of the English-speaking,[3] which is not surprising since they are in process of absorbing western civilisation, which the Whites have borne. The cinema seems to have been a major influence in this respect. The apparent result is that social standing among the African intelligentsia has depended largely upon the degree to which the dress, fashions, bearing and conduct of the Whites have been admired and borrowed.

There is an almost exact parallel in class prejudice. The poorer classes in countries of homogeneous population may envy and be taught to hate the middle classes and the rich, especially if politicians play on their acquisitive instincts. It is often easy to foster jealousy against those whose clothes, living environment, education, speech, manners, dignity, self-assurance and ability to command respect are accepted

---

[1] In comparison with Africans, the Coloureds are privileged. The latter may live under more pleasant circumstances, in less unpleasant districts and nearer to their work; they do not have to carry passes; they are not liable to be 'endorsed out'; and they have some chance, at least, of getting apprenticed. Nevertheless, because they belong culturally among the Whites (they are mainly Afrikaans-speaking) I regard the Coloureds as the most unjustly treated group in the Republic.

[2] On the other hand, a sense of injustice against the Whites certainly does exist among all non-Whites; it tends to be directed indiscriminately against the Whites, particularly by the Africans; politicians of whatever colour are inclined to foster and exploit this resentment and fan it into race hatred; and it has been the apparent inspiration of the resistant Poqo movement which, as I write, is being ruthlessly suppressed.

[3] Compare Wilson and Mafeje, *Langa*, p. 146: 'English carries status rather than Afrikaans, and the educated people think of it as the lifeline linking Langa with the outside world'.

as superior. But the classes which resent the higher social standing of others normally welcome rather than avoid friendships or contacts among those of higher station. They like to associate with people who, by reason of luck or merit, move in the upper circles.

But when Whites form the dominant class, it is not very easy for the more meritorious and able among the non-Whites to progress far in social prestige and esteem, even within their own group. One reason lies in the fact that the more successful among all the non-white races – Coloureds, Asiatics and Africans – are inclined to emulate the dominant white races. They are not content with rank in their own group. They may inhibit their feelings but they want to associate with their white equals in intellectual achievement and responsibility. This is all too often denied; yet is it not all too likely that, in this very human attitude, we have the origin of the intense bitterness which has emerged among so many of the leaders of the non-Whites? And does it not suggest that, even if it were otherwise practicable, no policy of 'separate development' would be likely to offer a solution?

ECONOMIC PRIVILEGE THE CAUSE OF DISCRIMINATION
We do not, however, find in colour prejudice as such the main origin – nor, perhaps, even the most important cause – of most economic colour bars. The chief source of colour discrimination is, I suggest, to be found in the natural determination to defend economic privilege (the preservation of 'customary economic relationships between the races'), non-Whites simply happening to be the essentially underprivileged groups in South Africa. Certainly colour custom and colour prejudice have been persistently exploited in efforts to win electoral support for measures which seek to curb the tendency of the profit system to admit the poorer races to better opportunities; but such casuistic exploitation of custom and prejudice does not make it the prime motive for the exclusion of competition from the despised or feared Coloureds, Asiatics or Africans. It resembles, indeed, the incitements which, in countries of homogeneous population, are so often exploited by trade union leaders in order to arouse those organised in 'closed

shops' to hostility against interlopers – the unapprenticed or 'unqualified'.

The naturalness of the fear of competition which the dissolution of colour privilege threatens is emphasised by the attitude of many of the Coloured community of South Africa when they feel that they may have to meet competition from Africans. In my judgment, the Coloured people have had the greatest cause to complain of unfair discrimination in their country. Yet, as Mr. G. V. Doxey has correctly reported,

> 'while on the one hand they [the Coloured people] have sought equality of opportunity with the white man, the majority of them, in turn, refuse to see the need for the same treatment to be given to the African population'.[1]

The present government has tried, not entirely without success, to obtain the support of some of the Coloured leaders for its *apartheid* policy by capitalising on the apprehensions of so many of the Coloured people that they may be reduced to the standards of the despised Africans.[2]

Lurking in the background of the complex of custom and prejudice which the power of the state has been used to appease is genuine alarm at the prospect of ultimate domination of the Africans in the political sphere, with spoliation of the Whites. These misgivings cannot be dismissed as illusory. They may not justify the means adopted to protect the future of the white minority, but they do, at any rate, help to explain it. And although the natural fears of the Whites have been exploited by machiavellian politicians concerned mainly with winning the votes of a badly misinformed and indoctrinated electorate, the fears themselves are wholly well-founded. The determination to preserve 'white civilisation' is not ignoble. But the unwillingness to share it is incapable of defence and the methods used expose that 'civilisation' to contempt. It is the cause

---

[1] *The Industrial Colour Bar in South Africa*, O.U.P., 1961, p. 99.
[2] In fact, increasing African employment has been essential for the rise in the real earnings of the Coloured people themselves over the last few decades. Without it, the industrial growth which has occurred in the Western Cape, and which has raised their average standards of living so rapidly and remarkably, could never have taken place.

of resentment among the non-Whites. And it is the consequence both of colour prejudice and of the not unfounded fear of ultimate domination by the Blacks.

But if we do not find in colour prejudice the chief incentive for legislative or collusively enforced colour bars, we do find in the consequences of economic exclusiveness a cause for the persistence of irrational race prejudice. I argue later that in a free economic system the rising economic standards of the non-Whites would have led to a gradual dissolution of prejudice, following periods of unavailing resistance, intransigence, disillusion and finally reappraisal of the realities of a changing world.

The effect of a sudden improvement in the material well-being of a socially subordinate race seems to be at first the intensification of prejudice. Thus, it often angers the poorer Whites in South Africa to see well-dressed Africans, or to hear them speak in a cultured manner. They regard it as presumption, as the assertion of a spurious claim to a higher social status. But an 'equality of aspect' which persists for any length of time slowly promotes social respect unless propaganda successfully prevents the abandonment of traditional attitudes.

A serious difficulty confronted in any attempt to interpret experience of race relations arises out of a tendency for resentments aroused by unquestionable injustices, as I have defined them, to be directed against wholly innocent parties, through whose agency unjust discriminations happen to be applied. For instance, Africans are apt to blame the officials whose duty it is to enforce the pass laws or influx control for the decisions required by those controls or laws.[1] Again, 'when fares are raised or transport inadequate . . . the crews are liable to be treated as scapegoats'.[2] Equally irrationally, the Africans tend to blame 'employers' for the relatively low wage-rates they can command rather than the legal enactments (such as the Wage and Industrial Conciliation Acts),

---

[1] I do not suggest that Africans (in the Republic of South Africa) have not frequently had good cause for feeling resentment against the police or other officials who have had to administer obnoxious laws as well as against the laws themselves.

[2] Wilson and Mafeje, *op. cit.*, p. 148.

social institutions (such as labour unions), or the customs which are responsible.

EXPLOITING INTOLERANCE TO PRESERVE INFERIORITY

If we are to consider all these issues in fair perspective, it is essential also that we shall continuously remind ourselves of how intolerant we human beings all tend to be, even within racially homogeneous communities, of groups who differ from us in status, speech or custom. This intolerance is greatly magnified when the other group appears to be rising or even aspiring to rise in status relatively to ourselves. Thus, urban Africans tend to speak disparagingly of the 'uskuse me' class – their intelligentsia or middle class, the more cultured, better dressed group among them. Subtle feelings of envy and the urge to see the relative status of one's group preserved account for such resentments. Naturally, these factors complicate the race-engendered irritations and tensions which contribute to feelings of colour injustice.

The broad conclusion suggested, which the following chapters will illustrate, is that the survival of colour prejudice is more a consequence than a cause of economic colour discrimination and injustice. But demagogic exploitation of the moral weaknesses from which all races suffer has perpetuated restraints on the competition of the non-Whites and thereby maintained them in a position of economic inferiority.

There are some who believe that the origins of the economic injustices perpetrated in the name of *apartheid* lie in deep, innate racial incompatibilities, explicable only by the social psychologists and anthropologists. Of course, psychological and anthropological factors cannot be ignored in any attempt to understand the problems of South Africa. But those who have observed, as I have, the natural friendliness of children of vastly different colours and racial characteristics playing happily together unless reprimanded by their parents and teachers, are unable to regard colour antipathies as *inherent* human characteristics. After 36 years of observation, I have been led to believe that colour prejudice has persisted through economic factors – through the perpetuation of the economic inferiority of the non-white peoples. In the pages which follow, I shall try to explain why I regard the economic colour discriminations in the Republic as an independent cause rather than a symptom of colour injustices.

CHAPTER 4

THE POOR WHITES

THE earlier economic backwardness of the Afrikaners in relation to the comparatively prosperous English-speaking section of the South African population contributed to anti-British resentment. In this Chapter it is proposed to consider briefly the reasons for the persistence of relative poverty among the Afrikaners during this century, and the feelings of injustice which it created. The Poor White problem – mainly the poor Afrikaner problem – appeared to be the product of a familiar phase of emergent industrialism which is rather inappropriately known as 'the drift to the towns', a phenomenon which we must view in perspective.

ATTRACTION TO TOWNS

The rise in the economic, social and health standards of the people during the 18th and early 19th centuries in Britain necessitated the creation of town proletariats. It created thereby unprecedented community circumstances and hence new problems,[1] and seemed to engender social evils as less conspicuous older evils were dissolved by the process. Likewise, the influx to the South African urban areas (of Coloureds and Africans, as well as of Whites) precipitated novel sociological problems, especially during the first 25 years of this century, as it raised the material well-being and aspirations of the majority. Matters such as housing, policing, sanitation, health and education had to be considered under circumstances in which previous experience could give relatively little guidance. Nevertheless, there is one vital difference between British experience under the *laissez-faire* background of the industrial revolution and South African experience under the relatively collectivist mentality of the present century. Whereas developing capitalism during the 18th and 19th centuries released

---

[1]For a balanced study of the problems of the large 18th century towns, see M. D. George, *London Life in the 18th Century*, Kegan Paul, 1925.

unparalleled equality of opportunity ('never were the barriers so down', says a leading historian of the age),[1] in South Africa the egalitarian forces of the free market were deliberately suppressed for the Coloureds, Indians and Africans.

The drift to the towns may be said to have begun in South Africa as the great mining regions opened and grew, with co-operant industries to serve them.[2] The great flow of people, white and black, first to the mining areas and later to the secondary industrial and trading regions, was hardly a 'drift'. Only the most powerful attracting or expelling forces could have led the custom-bound, conservative country dwellers to uproot themselves from their farms and rural village communities. But while the new urban areas seemed to offer much higher immediate standards of living and even more promising prospects, the rural areas were offering declining *relative* incomes and inferior prospects to all but the inheritors of farms.

It is common to describe the 'expelling force' as 'rural impoverishment'. That is rather misleading. It leaves an impression of falling *absolute* average standards of living on the part of white rural dwellers; but there is much evidence to suggest that this was not really the case. What did happen was that the *comparative* standards of living of the rural population fell, that is, in relation to urban communities. The maintenance of rural standards was largely due, of course, to the outflow, which was an expression of free choice by both the non-Whites and the Whites who migrated.[3] The 'expelling forces' and the 'attracting forces' were, on the whole, one and the same – the *relative* advantageousness and productiveness of urban life and pursuits.[4]

---

[1] M. C. Buer, *Health, Wealth and Population in the Early Days of the Industrial Revolution*, Routledge, 1926, p. 39.
[2] Whilst the population of South Africa as a whole has doubled since the beginning of the century, the urban population has increased five-fold.
[3] The poll tax on Africans implies some qualification of this assertion. The purpose was, in part, to force them to seek wage-paid employment outside the reserves.
[4] In the Cape Province, the attraction of the Whites to the towns not only maintained the standards of those Whites who remained in the rural areas but almost certainly raised the standards of the poor rural Coloureds who had provided the bulk of farm labour. The mobility of the rural Coloureds was restricted by ignorance, custom and prejudice;

INABILITY TO ADAPT TO URBAN LIFE

The *urban* Poor White problem was a consequence of imperfect adjustment to the migration so induced. But the resulting apparent impoverishment among formerly rural Afrikaners did not mean that their average material standards were not almost universally higher than they could have been on the farms or in the villages of the countryside. Quite probably many had been misled about prospects and were bitterly disappointed in what they found the town could actually offer them as untrained Whites. Yet virtually none of the Afrikaner town dwellers returned permanently to the countryside, in spite of a natural nostalgia for the homes and playgrounds of their youth. Having once become accustomed to the urban environment, they had no real longing for the life which the material rewards they could expect on the farms were offering them; whilst they, and especially their children, were much better cared for than would have been possible in the rural districts.

But rural traditions (whether of the Afrikaners, the Coloureds, or the Africans) were badly adapted to urban life. The virtual illiteracy of so many of the Afrikaners who left the farms, their high birth rate, their habits of living, their trusting simplicity which made them easy prey to sharp practice, and their aversion to manual work (which they had been brought up to regard as the function of an inferior, non-white caste), gradually brought into being the urban 'Poor White' problem. The main features of this problem showed themselves very early in the mining era,

---

but there seems to be little doubt that, in the Cape, the relative scarcity of farm labour, caused by the departure of so many Whites, has progressively improved the rather low standards of the rural Coloureds. Growing resort to African labour for farm work in the Cape (which has increased African earnings) has mitigated the tendency to rural 'labour shortage', and may be thought to have worked in the opposite direction. But that inference would rest upon an unduly static view of the reactions. The increase in African employment on the Cape farms and recourse to labour-saving economies (including gradual mechanisation of some branches of farm work) has, through the operation of the 'Say Law', actually enhanced the marginal productivity of coloured labour and the Coloureds' real earnings. (In accordance with the 'Say Law', the demand for the product of labour in one field is increased through cheapening the product of labour in any non-competing field.)

but it began seriously to worry the community only after Union (in 1910) when unskilled Whites, and to a small extent unskilled Coloureds, flowed into the towns. It was the contrast in standards which prompted the misgivings.

The skilled artisan classes employed in industry and commerce consisted then mainly of persons with a European background (chiefly British) but including, in the Cape, certain groups of Coloured artisans. The rural Afrikaners who sought town employments not only lacked industrial skills initially; they seemed to have no powerful urge to acquire these skills, nor were they well adapted by experience and education for training in them. What was worse, after the First World War industrial legislation, particularly the Apprenticeship Act, stood in their way as a formidable legislative barrier.

The situation could probably have been mitigated if the newcomers had been eager to enter industry *via* simple labouring work, using such employment as an avenue for training in skilled operations.[1] But they had been taught to regard any form of labouring as 'Kaffir work' and hence as beneath the white man's dignity. Some commentators have suggested, for this reason, that at the root the Poor White problem was psychological. It took the form of a growing class of relatively impoverished Whites, resentful of their low social standing but unfit for any kind of urban employment other than that of overseer of unskilled African or Coloured labour; and there was a tendency for the earning ability of this class – unless subsidised in some way – to fall to that of the Coloured people, or even as low as that of the Africans.

These circumstances gave rise to the gravest forebodings until, in the 1930s, the problem seemed suddenly to solve itself. What had happened was that entrepreneurial ingenuities, under the profit incentive,[2] had broken through

---

[1] That this is possible is proved by many instances of Africans who have learned and (more or less surreptitiously) actually performed various kinds of skilled or responsible work in industry, after having become adapted to the industrial environment.

[2] This profit incentive was stimulated by the increased dollar price of gold brought about in 1934, and by the dynamic effects of the rapid economic integration of non-Whites in response to the labour scarcity created by the war effort of 1939–45.

some of the barriers of custom and law which had been restraining the more effective economic integration of the white and non-white races. In so doing, successful profit-seekers created – almost miraculously – opportunities for the absorption of the Poor Whites into relatively well-paid industrial or commercial occupations. The barriers had had their origin in tradition and prejudice, but they had survived through labour union pressures and measures such as the Wage Act, the Apprenticeship Act and the Industrial Conciliation Act. In Doxey's words:

> 'the concept of trade unionism, and, for that matter, of socialism', had gradually become 'accepted in the minds of European artisans as the means of maintaining their own position against non-white inroads.'[1]

The barriers were evaded through the effective search for profitable spheres of development in which neither labour unions nor legislation could prevent openings for well-paid employments being offered to non-Whites. For the success of efforts to find the cheapest labour available raised average real wages for labour generally and – without subsidy – attracted even the Poor Whites into commerce and industry.

ECONOMIC INTEGRATION OF THE POOR WHITES

It was racial integration, which official policy always discouraged or actively opposed, that activated the economic expansion through which the Poor White problem has largely disappeared.[2] And it was market forces which provided the powerful incentives for those ingenuities which succeeded in evading the demand-destroying industrial segregation that legislative restraints were trying to enforce.[3]

Moreover, the same factors which, by providing opportunities for non-white advancement, created the real income flow that demanded the formerly Poor Whites' services,

---

[1] Doxey, *op. cit.*, pp. 23–24.
[2] Some aspects of the problem remain. The Minister of Transport recently declared that 10,000 to 11,000 Whites who are employed on the state railways are in fact so employed in order to prevent them from becoming a burden on the community. He could have added, 10,000 to 11,000 voters, who may be expected to support any political party which can be trusted to pay them most at the community's expense.
[3] See Chapter 9.

reacted more directly in dissolving the immediate barriers to the absorption of these initially unskilled white workers. The new industries and trades (unprotected at the outset by labour unions) gave easy access to industrial and commercial employments for Afrikaners of both sexes who had previously been excluded by apprenticeship requirements, the standard rate principle and the closed shop. But the basic cause of the astonishing solution of what had previously appeared to be a completely intractable problem was the increased contribution to the source of real income created by the industrial employment of previously excluded races.

Unfortunately, whilst the economic integration of races largely mitigated poverty problems, particularly among the Whites, it exacerbated the sociological problems created by fears of non-white competitors and the aversion of the Whites to social contact with non-Whites. It was these factors which had originally led, first, to attempts to preserve white standards, and second, to attempts to ensure the permanence of non-white inferiority (because it was felt that any economic 'levelling up' would inevitably lead to demands for social equality and equality of treatment in all respects).

CHAPTER 5

INJUSTICES TO AFRIKANERS

IN ANY study of colour injustice in the Republic of South Africa, it is essential to explain the traditional, but by no means unchanging, colour attitudes of the Afrikaners; for the nearly universally condemned *apartheid* policy has come to be identified with a government which represents especially (but not entirely) the Afrikaner voters.

STEREOTYPES AND DOGMA

Whilst attempting this task, I have been worried by the difficulty of dealing fairly, objectively yet succinctly with this question. In ordinary social life the Afrikaners are, like the white Americans of the 'deep South', a generous, hospitable, kindly, honourable and courageous people, for whom I have the most genuine regard. For themselves, they have created over the years a way of life which many would describe as a good society, in the best sense of that term. Within their group they constitute a virtually classless community, great differences of income, education and breeding not having given rise to the more obvious forms of snobbery. Their cultured élite – whose literary achievements are, in my judgment, impressive – are deeply attached to their language which, even now, they feel is in danger of being swamped by English. The emotions so aroused have become a powerful factor in politics and have encouraged the élite to identify themselves with the Afrikaners as a whole and to accept the stereotypes of the masses uncritically, especially in religious and colour issues.

Until recently, the Afrikaner intelligentsia have, I think, felt compelled to be loyal to, rather than to claim the loyalty of, the rank and file of their own people. They have seemed reluctant to undertake the formidable task of constructive leadership through a dangerous era. The long inculcated, obstinately held tenets and dogma of the Afrikaner populace have been crying out for adjustment to the realities of a shrinking world; but their trusted leaders seem to have been caught in the dilemma that any attempt to disturb the stereotypes of the majority would threaten to undermine the trust on which they had always relied for their power to lead. This dilemma has confronted not merely the Afrikaner *literati*, but the politicians; and only in the last few years has there been clear evidence that the 'winds of change' have been causing statesmen, editors and predikants (clergy of the Dutch Reformed Churches) deliberately to attempt to modify (without weakening voting loyalty) some of the basic convictions of 'the Afrikaner nation.'

To develop this thesis effectively and show its relation to apparent colour injustice in the Republic, I must run the risk of offending many Afrikaner friends whom I would not wish to offend. If I tried to avoid giving offence I should weaken the clarity and objectivity at which I am aiming.

Races which grumble about the 'injustices' or 'oppressions' to which they are subjected can often be observed to be inflicting not dissimilar injustices upon other races. We find a very clear case of this in any study of the grievances of the Afrikaners against 'British imperialism' and their fight against the threat of 'Anglicisation'. In their policies towards the non-Whites, they are inflicting injustices which are remarkably similar to those of which they themselves have complained.

Following the British occupation of the Cape in 1806, official policy was more or less in conformity with the liberal ideals of the early 19th century – acceptance of the common rights of man and (the true hall-mark of British colonialism) an antipathy to any form of domination. I have already referred to the retention of Roman Dutch Law, Dutch institutions and tolerance of the Dutch language (Afrikaans) as it had developed in the Cape. This expression of European liberalism was, however, anathema to the settled Dutch community as a guide to the attitude to be taken towards the non-white races. The Afrikaners, mainly descendants of the Dutch, had quite naturally developed rigid sociopsychological attitudes during a régime in which the nonWhites (slave or free) constituted an inferior caste destined to do all the heavy, unskilled manual work. The attitude so acquired tended to be strengthened by the teachings in South Africa of the Dutch Reformed Churches. The Afrikaner, who had long been isolated from European influences, was encouraged to cling to the ancient superstitions, long discarded in most other creeds, which associate white with goodness and purity, and black with sin, evil, dirt and death.[1] His naïve sincerity on this issue has tended to sanctify for him what would otherwise appear as an unchristian and unashamed discrimination against those of non-white skin pigmentation.

RELIGION AND POLITICS

As a religious doctrine the Afrikaner form of Calvinism, preached by the Dutch Reformed Churches in South Africa, is dominated by the idea of predestination and original sin. The Afrikaners have been taught to believe that in maintaining the subordinacy of the non-Whites they are fulfilling the will of God. Their churches have taught that policies (both economic and political) which have appeared incidentally to serve the short-term material interests of the white man are sanctioned by the highest moral law; and further that it is the duty of the state to use its power for this great purpose without inhibition.[2]

I do not suggest that all the Afrikaner leaders have shared these comfortable ethical convictions. But the Calvinistic churches of South Africa have, as a result of history, become almost as completely subservient to a political party, the Nationalist Party, as the exponents of Marxism appear to be to the Communist parties behind the Iron Curtain. The occasional protests of a few courageous predikants and mounting uneasiness within their churches merely high-

---

[1] A student of mine who has been conducting research into the changing purchasing patterns of the urban Afrikaner reports that, for this reason, white fish and chicken – 'especially the white meat' – are regarded as 'extremely suitable for invalids and children'.

[2] A resolution of the World Council of Churches of 1960, to the effect that 'no man who believes in Christ may be excluded from any church on the grounds of his race or colour', was explicitly rejected at all five synods of the Dutch Reformed Church in 1961, and the Church left the World Council.

light a necessary qualification of my assertion.[1] But very nearly the full power of the Afrikaner churches has been used for the benefit of the Party. Not only do they pray for victory at elections, but afterwards, when there has been a victory for the Party, there have actually been prayer meetings to thank the Almighty for having answered their supplications.

A powerful influence in ensuring that the Afrikaners' religious institutions shall serve the Party seems to be the activities of a secret society known as the Broederbond. Members of this society, bound by a disciplined secrecy, are believed to have obtained all the key posts in the three Calvinist churches,[2] and more than 40 per cent of the predikants are believed to belong either to the Bond directly or to its subsidiary, the Ruiterwag.[3]

The Afrikaner's conservatism—his bondage to attitudes, ways of thinking and modes of living which had developed in the insularity of remote farms and the small villages of

---

[1] An anti-*apartheid* stand by Professor A. S. Geyser of the Nederluitse Hervormde Kerk (one of the major Dutch Reformed Churches) who lectured on theology at the University of Pretoria, led to a recent heresy trial at which he was found guilty and unfrocked. He was reinstated after a successful appeal to the Supreme Court.

A recently started monthly religious journal, *Pro Veritate*, edited by the Rev. C. F. B. Naudé, presents a different interpretation of the scriptures. There is no doubt that many predikants are deeply embarrassed on the race issue. A motion introduced at a synod in October, 1962, demanding disciplinary action against clergy 'who do not show the necessary loyalty towards synodal decisions which lay down policy on racial matters' was not put to the gathering.

[2] In a recent pamphlet entitled *Church and Secret Organisation*, Professor A. van Selms (head of the Department of Semitic Languages at the University of Pretoria) says that Broederbond members of the Church are subject to secret decisions taken before meetings. Consultation, therefore, serves no purpose. On the secrecy factor he comments: 'It has happened that people have told me they are Freemasons, but it has never happened that someone has told me he is a member of the Broederbond'.

[3] The Ruiterwag is a 'Youth Wing'. The Communist parallel is obvious. It is widely rumoured also, in spite of emphatic government denials, that the Broederbond is the controlling influence in determining promotions in the public service, whilst the Ruiterwag is said to have acquired effective control over the composition of students' representative councils in the Afrikaans language universities. The methods used against independent-minded Afrikaners are said to be whispering and smearing campaigns.

the back-veld – together with the isolating factor of his language (which has often given poor access to the ideas of the contemporary world) have, in the whole course of this century's history, hindered his assimilation into the rapidly modernising agricultural and industrial economies of the present age.

What aggravated the disadvantages from which the Afrikaner suffered for these reasons was the political success of the Party which had won his allegiance. There was genuine sentiment in the desire to retain Afrikaans as a living language and the desire to avoid 'Anglicisation', by which was meant the gradual relinquishment of typical Afrikaner characteristics. But what most of their leaders termed 'Anglicisation' meant nothing more than their adaptation to the emerging era. Moreover, the organisers of the Nationalist Party, which has exploited Afrikaner sentiment, appear to have perceived shrewdly that the general backwardness of their supporters facilitated the task of vote-winning. Skilful political leaders found it profitable tactics to create and maintain an exclusive Afrikaner group, 'die Boerenasie'. This group was persuaded to regard itself as engaged in a life and death struggle against 'Anglicisation', a 'backs-to-the-wall struggle' to preserve its language and traditions. A disciplined allegiance was therefore demanded of its members, an allegiance which amounted almost to a naïve subservience on the part of the grievance-fed, ill-informed Afrikaner masses.

SEGREGATION OF AFRIKAANS AND ENGLISH

One of the most effective means of preserving the atmosphere of a fight for survival was that of preventing the growth of mutual respect and understanding between the English- and Afrikaans-speaking sections. This has been achieved throughout largely by the segregation of the two groups during their school years. The widespread wish of the English-speaking section to create a truly bi-lingual nation, through dual medium schools, was bitterly and successfully opposed. In the Transvaal, the complete separation of Afrikaans- and English-speaking children in schools was fortified by the removal from parents of the right to determine in which language their children should receive school instruction. Yet the root dissensions between the two white groups have for long been wholly superficial. The gulf remains formidable only because it is still thought to be politically important to perpetuate it, and because continuous effort has been devoted to this end.[1]

The pity of it is that the circumstances which the Afrikaner was persuaded to regard as unjust were partly of his own wholly innocent creation,[2] and partly the not so innocent fault of political leaders who, in the process of bidding for votes, have fostered grievances and hostility to the English-speaking section. The Party leaders wanted to prevent and succeeded in preventing the rank and file of their supporters from sharing in European culture and European values, in much the same way that attempts are now being made – for quite different reasons – to discourage the Transkei Africans from becoming 'Europeanised', by making Xhosa an official language for that area.[3]

I know of no legal or collusively imposed restraints to the disadvantage of the Afrikaners; and in so far as sheer prejudice on the part of the English-speaking managements of private firms may have meant injustice to them, that prejudice was of a kind which would have dissolved rapidly under the pressures of the free market, if they had been encouraged by their leaders to prepare themselves for the modern world.

RELIGIOUS APPROVAL OF RACIAL POLICY
In their efforts to maintain the subjection or the subordinacy of the non-Whites, the Nationalist Afrikaners have been able to use methods of which Afrikaner Calvinism has tended

---

[1] It is for this reason that television has not been permitted in the Republic.
[2] We can take two parallels. The Indian community of South Africa would have progressed economically very much more over the last three decades if their traditions had not frowned so strongly upon the employment of women. Similarly, the Africans could well have benefited considerably had they resisted less stubbornly attempts to encourage them to grow and consume more nutritious kinds of food. The 'blame', if 'blame' is the correct word, in these cases lies in traditions and, in the case of the Africans, in the complex psychological factors which determine food choice.
[3] See Chapter 17, pp. 165-6.

to approve. Professor H. M. Robertson of the University of Cape Town has recently pointed out that the Afrikaner Calvinist tends 'to be consciously anti-capitalistic, the "capitalist spirit" virtually being regarded as idolatry.'[1] He quotes in this connection a contribution made by a well-known Afrikaner to a symposium published by the Federation of Calvinistic Student Unions in South Africa which argues that '... Socialism is a justified reaction against the abuses of capitalism ...' I shall be showing that this is essentially because the Calvinists in South Africa have thought in terms of an established order based upon non-Whites being the hewers of wood and drawers of water, an order which 'capitalism' has always appeared to be disturbing. When Afrikaners refer to the 'abuses of capitalism' they think of its lack of respect for privilege and historically determined race and class structures; and they think of the latter as having been more or less heaven-ordained.

It is an ironic comment on the politics of this century that the 'Liberal' British Government which won the 1906 general election largely on the allegation (quite false) of 'Chinese slavery' in the South African mines should, as one of its first acts, have granted self-government to the Transvaal, whose rulers in church and state believed in the inherent inferiority of non-Whites and their right and duty to maintain the supremacy of the Whites.

---

[1] 'Marx, Menger, Mercantilism and Max Weber', in *Studi in Onore di Anitore Fanfani*, Vol. VI, 1962.

APPENDIX TO CHAPTER 5

'CHINESE SLAVERY'

THE facts about 'Chinese slavery' are, briefly, as follows. During the Boer War, the bulk of the Africans who, as we shall see, had provided the larger part of mining labour, ceased to trek to the mines for employment. The habit thus disturbed took a long time to restore.[1] Under those conditions, resort to indentured labour was essential for the recovery of gold-mining (a recovery which was, incidentally, to the advantage of the whole South African economy, and especially of the poorest classes). Accordingly, 50,000 indentured Chinese labourers were recruited to overcome the serious shortage of African labour.

The Chinese themselves certainly did not welcome their forced repatriation from 1907. From their point of view they were being sacked from their jobs for political reasons.[2] But hardly anyone in Britain worried about the 50,000 Chinese who had been thrown out of an employment they did not want to leave and deported. They had been rescued from 'slavery', and the conscience of the self-righteous British voters was satisfied.

The next step of the 'Liberal' British Government which had been responsible for this noble action was to grant self-government to the Transvaal, where the whole political and religious tradition was known (by the politicians, not the British voters) to have been based on the principle of 'no equality between Black and White'. Of course, the British 'Liberals' were wholly well-intentioned. They sincerely thought they were restoring rights to the poor, simple, pious Boers, who had been innocent victims of Chamberlain's imperialism.[3] But the Boers made no secret of their intention

---
[1] I discuss the reasons in Chapter 6, pp. 54-5.
[2] As their contracts ran out.
[3] In case I should be misunderstood, I must explain that I deplore the policies of Chamberlain, Rhodes and Jameson at least as much as the equally deplorable mis-rule and corruption of the Kruger regime.

to perpetuate the subordination of the non-Whites. And, after Union, methods were immediately adopted (at first in 1911) which restrained developments (mainly in mining) which at that time were threatening to facilitate the economic advance of the African.

If the 'Liberal' British Government had been more interested in the welfare of the unrepresented non-Whites of South Africa for whom it still held responsibility, it could have insisted upon a full and careful enquiry into the future economic and political rights of non-Whites before handing over political power to the Boers. But it would have been politically dangerous for it to have adopted any form of policy which conflicted with the 'Liberal' electorate's stereotypes about 'Chinese slaves', the South African mines, or the deeply-wronged, Christian Boers.

CHAPTER 6

AFRICANS IN THE MINES

TRIBAL BACKGROUND

TO understand the position of the Africans in the economy of South Africa and the rights and wrongs of the system, it is essential to know something of their tribal institutions and the attitudes formed in their homelands – 'the reserves'. These tribal influences, although in process of adaptation, and indeed disintegration, are still powerful, even among many of those Africans who spend most of their time away from their tribe.[1] However indefensible or unwise South African policy has been in its dealings with the Africans, it has usually had the virtue of taking account of their primitive background. Unfortunately, it is impossible to deal adequately, in a book of this kind, with the issues which arise when a primitive race, sociologically isolated by tradition, law and collusive action, has become an integral part of a modern, highly progressive economy. These are important aspects of the relations between the Whites and the Blacks which I shall be unable to discuss. Nevertheless, I hope to make clear the reasons for African feelings of injustice which have recently been so successfully exploited as to goad the Government to the most drastic repressive measures.

WAGE OPPORTUNITIES IN MINING

We must begin with a brief sketch of the way the Africans were increasingly attracted since the last century, mainly as unskilled labourers, into the white man's economy, until today two-thirds of the black races can find subsistence only by working outside the reserves (the areas in which a modified tribal system still prevails).

Africans were attracted from the reserves last century

---

[1] Opinions differ about the proportion which could be properly described as fully detribalised. See Chapter 10, pp. 87-9.

through what seemed to them to be almost unbelievably favourable opportunities and prospects of improving their material condition. It was the rise of the great areas of mining activity which created these prospects. At the same time, the incentives for Africans to accept employment in the mines were strengthened by signs of increasing privation in the tribal areas due to soil erosion, population growth, and extending land occupation by Whites.

In the rough, early years of diamond activity, which constituted the pioneer development of mining in South Africa, the labour of the Africans, however unskilled, was at first in such demand that the wage-rates of black labourers sometimes rose nearly as high as those paid to white overseers. But even in an imperfect market, knowledge of mining employment opportunities spread in the tribal regions so that, despite the increasing demand for labour through the beginnings of gold-mining development, a growing inflow of unskilled Africans had by the middle 1880s brought down the market price for black labour to a small proportion of the rate needed to attract Whites. This disparity persisted through the gold-mining era and has lasted (for non-market reasons) until today. It had originally been thought essential, and was later felt to be appropriate, to employ Whites to supervise the operations of the raw African labourers. Since the alternative employments open to the Whites in farm and rural areas, although possibly declining as the 19th century advanced, were nevertheless very much more favourable than those open to Africans, supply and demand appears to have forced a wide discrepancy in the middle 1880s. Wage-rates for the white supervisors – untutored as they usually were – had yet to be very much higher than those required to attract African labour.

This was partly because, through organised recruitment and word of mouth, an understanding of the remuneration offered to Africans permeated the kraals (villages). The recruiting machinery which the mines soon found it profitable to set up actively informed the tribal communities of the opportunities which the mines were providing. It has been alleged that their agents painted at times an unduly rosy picture of the advantages, amounting sometimes to fraudulent persuasion, but African labourers who had once experienced mining work returned voluntarily again and again after their customary periodic sojourn with their family and tribe. Indeed, it soon became a mark of status or prestige within the tribe to have served in the mines.

In stressing the disparities which emerged between the earnings of Whites and Blacks, I am not alleging an unjust absolute level of remuneration. The earnings of Africans in South Africa have never been as low, in real terms, as they are commonly believed to have been. In this century, however, African wage-rates have been influenced through the only unquestionable instance of a labour-purchasing monopsony of which I know, that of a common recruiting organisation for all the mines. It has had the effect of ensuring a larger and more regular labour supply by overcoming the high 'leisure preference' of Africans,[1] rather than the effect of 'exploiting' labour.

AFRICANS' HIGH 'LEISURE PREFERENCE'

The unacquisitive nature of tribal Africans, possibly because the accumulation of private property (except in the form of cattle) offends the 'communistic' psychology of aboriginal societies, has, from the beginning, created one of the major difficulties of mining management. Moreover, the conventional material needs of the Africans are low relatively to their earnings, so contributing to what has been called their 'wantlessness' or what I prefer to call high 'leisure preference'. Accordingly, those who found it profitable to employ them tried to find methods of increasing their preference for material goods as against 'leisure'. The morally least defensible way of attempting this was by means of poll taxes intended to force the Africans to earn the necessary money,[2] which they could only do by serving the

---

[1] See S. T. van der Horst, *Native Labour in South Africa*, O.U.P., 1942, pp. 128-138, 192-214.
[2] Under the Transvaal Labour Tax system, work performed for the State or for farmers was a method of settling the tax liability without money. The poll tax may be defended in principle, however, if it can be shown to be a relatively cheaply administered means of raising revenue to pay for collective objectives, if the rapid achievement of higher material standards by all is accepted as one of these collective objectives, or if the intention is educative – the active discouragement of primitive indolence when employment opportunities are available.

white man outside the reserves, on the farms or mines or elsewhere. The monopsonistic method might be defended as 'educative'.

In considering the use by the gold mines of monopsonistic power, we must remember that they have not been monopolistic in the sense that they have ever organised to prevent the entry of additional capital or restrict the level of output. The price of gold has been beyond their control, and there has been freedom to invest in this highly speculative field as well as in complementary industries.[1] Moreover new development has competed freely for African labour, despite the common recruitment organisation. It is not surprising, therefore, that Professor S. Herbert Frankel found the average yield to investment in gold-mining to have been remarkably low,[2] before the currency devaluations of the 1930s, particularly the dollar devaluation of 1934, had produced an enormous windfall yield.

In the early mining days many Africans had to trek huge distances – literally hundreds of miles – on foot, involving weeks and sometimes months of almost incredible hardship. In the case of the gold mines the hardships were aggravated by the dangers of exploitation by Transvaal farmers demanding free labour in return for the right to pass over their land; forced labour imposed by governmental authority en route; extortion by the police and conventional robbery. The mining corporations did their best to get the Transvaal Government to tackle these abuses, due chiefly to maladministration, but without avail before the Boer war.[3] Yet, in spite of all these hardships and hazards, after short spells of work, originally for a few months and later for an average of a year or more, the Africans travelled back to their tribal

---

[1] Especially after the Boer war, when maladministration in the Transvaal, including the practice of granting private monopolies and concessions for the production or import of necessities, was brought to an end. Transport remains today the sole big exception. The mines have been seriously exploited through the railway tariff and, because the State-owned railways are protected against road motor traffic, they have no remedy.

[2] S. H. Frankel, *Capital Investment in South Africa*, pp. 79–80.

[3] Most of the abuses were brought to an end after the Boer war; and the common recruitment organisation has since provided private protection against the possibility of similar forms of maltreatment developing.

kraals with the firm intention of returning to the mines for further periods of employment.

Competing with the mines for African labour were the farms, owned for the most part by Afrikaners. Farm labour was remunerated largely in kind and through permission to dwell ('squat') on the farmer's land. Competition between the farms and the mines has been a continuous determinant of the remuneration which has had to be offered to attract the Africans to both fields of employment.

The cheapness of African labour did not, therefore, imply its 'exploitation'. Indeed, as we have seen, it was the rise in the Africans' money earnings above the value of those wants that could be satisfied by money expenditure, to which we can trace – in part – the origin of their high demand for leisure (the long periods devoted to living on previous earnings in the reserves).[1] Nor was their primitiveness a reason for the cheapness of their labour. Their reluctance to break with the traditions of their tribe, their bewilderment at having to work under the discipline of foreigners with an incomprehensible moral code and talking a strange language, the need for a regularity of activity quite unparalleled in their primitive background, and the need for periodic return to their wives and families – all these factors inevitably handicapped the recruiters, both in persuading Africans to accept mining employment for the first time and in persuading them to shorten their habitual periods of residence in the reserves. To draw the Africans into the compounds, the benefits from mining work had to be correspondingly enhanced. To blame the mining corporations for the low wage-rates (low, that is, in comparison with the earnings of other races in other kinds of work) would, therefore, be to blame a mitigating factor and not a cause. Mining development has been (directly and indirectly) the greatest single uplifting factor for the poorer races and classes in South Africa, and especially for the Africans.

On the other hand, population growth in the reserves, due mainly to an alleviation of primitive African poverty

---

[1] Their separation from their wives and families has now become the chief cause of what I have termed their 'high demand for leisure'. The migratory labour problem is discussed below, pp. 52–3, and in Chapter 10, pp. 90–3.

for which mining employment must be given credit, has certainly been a labour-cheapening factor. But the cheapness of this labour soon became essential for the very survival of the population it had indirectly called into being. And this cheapness grew even more essential in order to maintain the relatively complex patterns of consumption which slowly emerged; for wholly new products had gradually become conventional necessaries – even within the reserves – as the Africans began to understand more of the new world to which they had been attracted.

When the Africans first entered the sphere of mining employment, they usually constructed their own primitive shelter from materials provided by the management. But it soon became essential to house them in barracks or compounds, a solution which was practicable because their women-folk did not accompany them. Here, isolated from urban influences in the wider sense, they largely preserved their tribal traditions whilst serving first a 19th and then a 20th century economy.

THE COMPOUND SYSTEM

The compound system was originally felt to be necessary in the diamond mines to prevent the theft of diamonds, for which there was at one time a ready market in the nearby Afrikaner republics. The system seems then to have been recognised as a method of employing African labour which was socially and politically acceptable. By the 1890s it had been generally adopted in large-scale mining for diamonds, gold or coal (and later for non-ferrous metals and asbestos). Within the compounds the necessaries of life were sold by shops, or provided as part of remuneration (which made it unnecessary for the compound dwellers to go outside). The material and social well-being of the employees so housed was, on balance, undoubtedly enhanced by these arrangements: the shelter was appropriate; surroundings were cleaner and healthier than they could have been without the mines' initiative; access to alcoholic liquor (other than 'kaffir beer') was prevented (with the result that a common type of absenteeism was avoided); access to prostitutes was prevented; medical facilities were usually incomparably better than under any other practicable system; meals served as part of remuneration were carefully considered in the light of nutritional knowledge (at least during this century);[1] facilities for recreation were provided; social life and organised sport could develop and were encouraged by most managements.[2]

Judgments may differ on how far such advantages can be regarded as adequate compensation for the isolation of African labourers from the modern world they were serving, and from their families. But the social milieu of the compounds served as some substitute, albeit unsatisfactory, for the lack of family life, and provided a framework within which a communal life adapted to a period of transition could develop. The prosperity of the mines has always depended upon their ability to attract their African employees back for further spells of employment, and compound amenities and conditions, along with conditions of work, have been a vital factor. As we shall see, the lack of similar facilities for those employed in secondary industry has given rise to serious problems of physical and moral hygiene.

I am not in the least concerned to defend the motives of the financiers and adventurers who developed the diamond and gold mines and complementary industries. Among them were no doubt ruthless and unscrupulous characters. Others were certainly 'tough', as pioneers must be when fighting for big prizes against great risks in the face of what must frequently have appeared as insuperable difficulties. Yet through their initiative all classes in South Africa benefited materially.

Neither the shareholders nor the administrators of the mines were responsible for colour bars or the withholding of opportunities of advancement from Africans. On the contrary, as far as organised labour and politics allowed, the mining interests always tried to prevent restrictions on

---

[1] In diamond mining, however, it was always the policy to pay an all-inclusive money wage, leaving each employee free to purchase (within the compound) such food and other consumers' goods as he fancied and could afford. (See Doxey, *op. cit.*, p. 35.)

[2] The listing of these virtues must not leave an impression of idyllic conditions. The standards of the mass of Africans employed in mining, although continuously improving, remain primitive.

the scope of African employment. Of course, they would have wanted to safeguard the established expectations of their existing white employees, at least as a means of maintaining staff harmony during the transition; and opportunities for Africans in skilled work and in positions of responsibility could, accordingly, have been opened up only gradually. But had the great mining magnates been free to insist on their interests as investors and those of a vast number of smaller shareholders, they would have opened the door, by slow degrees, to African advancement.

The mines never exploited African labour in the bad sense, as legislation (inspired by organised labour and not uninfluenced by broad restrictionist ideologies) certainly did. The mines liberated new opportunities for all races and especially for the most backward. The only elements of coercion which may be said to have driven Africans to the mines are (a) the poll taxes (and these taxes were introduced more in response to pressures from farming than from mining interests) and (b) the common recruitment organisation (described above) which sought to offset the Africans' high 'leisure preference'.

THE MIRAGE OF SLAVERY

The attitude of the world towards the South African mining industry has been influenced, I think, by stereotypes formed during the 'Chinese slavery' agitation, to which I have already referred. It is important, therefore, that this incident should be seen in perspective. The shortage of African labour which caused the mines to seek indentured Chinese in the early years of the century seems to have been partly due to the way the Boer war led to the breaking down of customary limitations on the employment of Africans in other spheres. The evasion of obstacles to equality of opportunity (as between sexes, age groups and races) has been a typical consequence of periods of war and reconstruction. In the Transvaal, the additional and competing demand for African labour was augmented by the quite different colour attitude of the British authorities, who were in control for some time after the war. They did not share the Boers' race prejudices and did not hesitate to use African labour where it would be useful. The post-war shortage of mine labour so caused was aggravated also by memories of former maltreatment by the Transvaal authorities. Moreover, the relatively high wage-rates that attracted the tribal Africans into war-time occupations not only financed longer periods (in the reserves), away from wage-paid work but led to the feeling that similar wage-rates ought to be offered in the mines. These factors, together with abundant harvests in the reserves immediately after the war,[1] disappointed the expectations which had stimulated mining development.

The repatriation of the Chinese in 1907 would have affected the development of mining even more adversely but for a sharp recession at that time which led to the dismissal of large numbers of Africans from other forms of employment. Because there were no labour unions or government restraints on wage-rates[2] the mines provided an automatic solution of the unemployment problem, by offering an immediate alternative source of income.[3]

Those who have said that capitalists want to maintain a supply of 'cheap docile labour' misconceive the interests of entrepreneurs. Certainly the co-ordination of complex activities demands 'discipline', and there may be no harm in describing willingness to accept entrepreneurial commands (themselves subject to the stern discipline of the market) as 'docility'. But it does not mean passivity in face of injustice, which is what is usually implied. In a competitive society, entrepreneurs have every incentive to produce at least-cost, which means acquiring the services of people as well as of physical agents as cheaply as possible.[4]

---

[1] See Doxey, *op. cit.*, p. 57.
[2] See Chapter 11.
[3] I certainly do not suggest that the motive was generosity. But this does not affect the question of the efficiency of the unhampered market as a means to the maintenance of full employment.
[4] In more general and less misleading terms, this has meant seeking the achievement of each economic objective with a minimum sacrifice of alternative objectives. If every entrepreneur were able to pay the lowest wage-rates needed to acquire labour in the free market, not only would the dispersion of wage-rates between low and high levels be reduced to a minimum but the aggregate flow of wages would be maximised. Moreover, there is no reason to believe that, through such an economising of labour, the proportion of wages to other incomes in the division of the value of the product would be reduced.

MARKET INCENTIVE TO ADVANCEMENT

But the advantage of the services of people compared with the services of physical productive agents is that people are intelligent and capable of wielding complex tools, under co-ordinated direction, and with discretion. It was possible to abolish slavery in various parts of the world without counter-revolution to restore it, because the cost of the abolition was negative, in spite of the frantic but unenlightened opposition of so many slave owners. And in the modern world in which there is a vast market to be served, there is a most powerful motive to invest in human capital and train primitive people for operations which require intelligence, judgment and responsibility.

The tendency of the free market to create opportunities for skill-acquisition by Africans was emphasised by technological progress, constantly being brought about by the enterprise of mining managements. As more mining skills were transferred to machines, a growing proportion of semi-skilled labour was required, for which Africans could easily be trained.

But the ambitions aroused by the readiness of some Africans to rise above 'put and carry work' provoked demands from the Whites for the restraint of the profit motive. Their fear was that the search for low cost output was tending to bring about a rapid rise in the standards of the more able or enterprising members of a primitive people, and so threatened their relative status.

Whenever the point of view of the mine-owners was publicly expressed, it was clear that they were wholly in favour of opening the door to African advancement, through permitting the training of Africans for more productive and more valuable work – a policy which, they occasionally perceived, would tend ultimately to reduce race friction. Their motive of 'profit-seeking' or 'loss-avoidance' conflicted with the barriers to African skill-acquisition; for these barriers rendered the low-grade, marginal mines, and the low-grade seams in all mines, unprofitable. But they were invariably realistic in not suggesting revolutionary changes. They never envisaged more than a gradual relaxation of the colour bars which we are about to discuss. Yet they knew only too well that there was much semi-skilled work which was performed by Whites (at the traditional high wage-rates) which could have been efficiently performed by Africans after a period of training at wage-rates very much higher than were then available to Africans, but very much lower than were currently commanded by the Whites. The mines would have benefited handsomely if such a step could have been taken, and it would have prevented the emergence of one of the most conspicuous colour injustices in South Africa.

CHAPTER 7

THE FIRST COLOUR BAR ACT

A WIDE discrepancy between the earnings of Africans and the earnings of virtually unskilled white overseers seems to have been established as a tradition in the 1880s in the diamond mines. I have suggested that this discrepancy could be partly explained by the market forces of supply and demand. White supervisors were needed, whilst they had better-paid alternatives than the Africans.

In so far as the notion of what was a 'fair and proper' remuneration for a white man may have influenced the ratio during the early years of this century, it limited the scope for white employment in mining and so reduced the socially beneficial effects of mining development in mitigating the emerging Poor White problem. But new factors gradually became operative as the country advanced. Whilst the early mines had been relatively unsystematically exploited, later operations became more scientific, better organised and mechanised. The demand then was for ever-increasing expertness in artisans and intermediate management personnel. For such reasons the *average* productivity of Whites appears to have risen at least in proportion to that of Africans. Hence, wage comparisons for this century must allow for the fact that average wage-rates for the Whites cover not only the remuneration of virtually unskilled supervisory work, but that of highly skilled artisans, most of whom had to be attracted from abroad; whereas the remuneration of Africans, although it covers tasks of some responsibility and skill performed (sometimes more or less surreptitiously) by a small minority, is almost entirely for labouring tasks.

Because of the shortage of skilled personnel in South Africa at the beginning of the century, artisan immigrants, reared in the traditions of the emergent restrictionist ideologies and British trade unionism, were brought to fill artisan and foreman posts. It is hardly surprising that, after the Boer war (and together with their Afrikaner comrades after 1907), they should have endeavoured to enforce a sort of closed shop which denied all opportunities for advancement to their non-white comrades. The political background of the period had produced stereotypes which actively encouraged the formation of labour unions, and the strike power so created seems to have enabled the Whites to perpetuate the ratio of white to non-white wage-rates which had been established by the 1880s. In this way, the unions managed not only to preserve the remuneration of their members against the competition of their fellow Whites, but later to forbid the training of Africans for employment in responsible, supervisory and skilled occupations.

What was probably at that time the most blatant colour bar of history (although by no means the most burdensome) received the force of law in 1911. The motive was industrial peace; but it was sought *via* an appeasement of the militant white labour organisation, which appeared then to be growing in strike power and political support.

MILITANT WHITE TRADE UNIONISM

The beginnings of militant unionism date from the 1880s and 1890s when branches of British labour unions were opened in South Africa.[1] The leadership was in the hands of typical union officials of the British type – hard, ruthless but scarcely Marxist. Quite early in South African labour history, however, the influence of the extreme Left seems to have been discernible, and resort to violence in support of strike action was not uncommon. This tendency was probably due to infiltration of the class-war idea from foreign countries rather than from the relatively respectable British trade unionism of the day.

In the 1880s an organisation known as the Knights of Labour, which had its origin in the United States, seemed to be acquiring a following. Two of the leaders of the South

---

[1] The Amalgamated Society of Carpenters and Joiners was opened in 1881; the Amalgamated Society of Engineers in 1886. The first permanent purely South African labour union, the South African Typographical Union, apparently dates from 1898.

African branch were sentenced to eight months hard labour in 1890 for their part in a strike on the diamond mines which had led to bloodshed and the blowing up of the De Beers offices.

That same year a young Englishman from Suffolk, W. H. Andrews, a fitter by trade, joined the labour union movement. He was destined to become one of the chief leaders of the extreme Leftist or Marxist wing. Superficially, he gave the impression of being a typical industrial unionist, but in 1915 he broke with the Labour Party and formed the International Socialist League (a sort of South African ILP) and a few years later he became the first Secretary of the Communist Party in South Africa. He was concerned in several of the more violent strikes and is known to have taken part in a strike (which was ruthlessly crushed by Kruger) on the Randfontein gold mines in 1897. He remained active in aggressive unionism until the state took over from the labour unions the task of protecting white privilege.

After the Boer war, the prospects of militant unionism caused grave misgivings, particularly on the Rand. The Transvaal Miners Association (later the South African Mine Workers Union) was founded in 1902 and a successful strike on the Crown Reef Mine followed. The organisers of the labour unions were then persuaded by their extremist wing to think in political terms. In 1904 the first Labour Day demonstration took place in Johannesburg, and the Witwatersrand Trades and Labour Council was founded to provide rather loose machinery for the co-ordination of the different unions, and to undertake 'agitational work' with political aims.

In the early years of the century, contemporary French syndicalism seems to have fired the imagination of some of the South African labour leaders, and even the 'anarchist' American IWW (Industrial Workers of the World), which urged the use of the general strike to overthrow capitalism and did not hesitate to advocate violence, is thought to have played some part in the formation of ideologies – possibly through the influence of a fiery Scot named Norrie, who was chairman of the Social Democratic Federation. The history of strikes in the South African mines is remarkably similar to that in the American mines which the IWW organised during the same period.[1] In 1910, an IWW missionary named Webber visited South Africa;[2] but although some seeds were sown, the organisation itself never took root in South Africa. In 1919, however, another advocate of violent class war, Tom Mann, visited South Africa and addressed meetings for several months.

How far the ideas from all these sources were indirectly responsible for strike violence is uncertain.

In 1907, a turbulent strike occurred on the Rand mines. It involved some bloodshed[3] and much sabotage. The importance of this strike is that it prepared the way for colour bar legislation. The government of the day, that of Smuts and Botha, had obtained office with the support of the white miners who, up to that time, had been mainly of British origin. Nevertheless, the government seized the opportunity created by the strike to bring Afrikaners into the mines as trainee miners – i.e., as 'scabs' in the eyes of the Miners' Association. At the same time, almost as though the state felt the need for some compensating gesture towards the existing skilled miners, the Transvaal Ordinance No. 17 of 1907 was introduced to protect the Whites against skilled competition from the Chinese (many of whose employment contracts did not expire for a couple of years or more). Through this Ordinance a precedent for the two 'Colour Bar Acts' was created.

The following year a long and bitter strike – in which Andrews appears to have been the leading organiser – occurred at the Kimberley diamond mines. The next year there was another strike, caused by opposition to piece work in the workshops of the Natal Government Railway System. Again, Andrews appears to have been the leading spirit. And in 1911, a strike of Johannesburg tramwaymen took place leading to violence and allegations of attempted

---

[1] When the Transvaal Afrikaners came to constitute the bulk of the white miners, a cause of the similarity may be what F. R. Dulles (*Labour in America*, p. 209) calls 'the independent and often lawless spirit of the frontier'.

[2] Dr. the Hon. T. H. Boydell tells me that, in June 1910, he debated publicly with Webber.

[3] Two members of the Miners' Association executive were charged with murder, but the evidence was inconclusive and they were acquitted.

dynamiting which Andrews, who was again involved, claimed was a frame-up.

INDUSTRIAL COLOUR BAR TO APPEASE UNIONS

In these circumstances, it appears to have been thought politic, for the sake of harmony, to confer by law those privileges which white miners might otherwise have been encouraged to seek by strike action. It was felt that, unless Africans were excluded from opportunities by legislation, intermittent and violent private steps would be taken to enforce the exclusion. Against this background, the Mines and Works Act of 1911 (which has been aptly termed the 'Colour Bar Act') was passed. This legislative sanction for the colour bar was, however, a concession not only to socialist and labour union pressures, but equally an appeasement of Afrikaner sentiment.

Whilst the provisions of the Act were superficially innocuous, it authorised arbitrary governmental action through delegated legislation. The government was given power, in the interests of safety, to make regulations relating to the issue of certificates permitting certain kinds of work to be undertaken. But the regulations actually promulgated (against which it was thought there could be no appeal) provided that a large variety of mining occupations, which outside the former Boer republics (for example, in the Cape and Natal) could be performed by artisans of all races, could not legally be performed by Africans in the Transvaal and the Orange Free State. At the same time a ratio was specified between foremen (Whites) and mining labourers (Africans) who could be employed in the activities covered.[1]

The general secretary of the white workers' labour union, typically blaming 'the capitalist class', explained that whilst he was 'a Socialist as far as all the workers in the globe are concerned', he believed that his union had the right to fight against and oust the Africans if they were 'used as semi-slaves for the purpose of keeping others down'. The paradox

---
[1] If the Transvaal had been under British rule and administration from the outset, the old Cape tradition may well have prevented either the passing of the Mines and Works Act of 1911 or the regulations issued under it.

was that the employment of white miners depended upon what he called the 'semi-slavery ... of ... dirty, evil-smelling Kaffirs';[1] for without their unskilled work the great majority of the mines would have had to close. What he was in fact objecting to was the desire of 'the capitalist class' to achieve economies by bringing better remunerated and more responsible work within reach of the Africans. The fact that this would disturb the relative earnings of the skilled Whites appeared to him to be a sufficient justification for insistence upon the colour bar.[2]

One can sympathise with the mine workers, indoctrinated against 'the capitalist'. They felt, sincerely enough, that their privileged position was precarious by reason of the search for profits. At the same time, they were unprepared to permit any form of levelling up because it would have threatened their relative status. If the earnings of the 'dirty Kaffirs' rose, it was essential, they felt, that their earnings should rise at least in proportion to preserve their self-respect as white men. The most virulent among the white miners seem to have been those who had not troubled to qualify themselves for promotion. Their highly paid status had come to depend not upon their qualifications but upon their power, through union action and political pressure, to exclude African competition.[3]

---

[1] Quoted in Doxey, *op. cit.*, pp. 118–119.
[2] At times, the labour union argument against permitting the Africans to progress was that they were *incapable* of taking responsibility and handling complex mechanical tools. But if that had been true they could have expected the mine-owners to stand with them on this issue.
[3] On the Rhodesian copper belt, where the privileges of the 7,000 white miners have been protected solely by the formidable power of their labour union, the absence of any legal colour bar has meant that more than 2,000 Africans have succeeded (very gradually) in getting employment of an order of skill and responsibility which would never have been permitted in the Republic of South Africa, although there has been nothing yet resembling equality of opportunity. The recent achievement of independence by Northern Rhodesia is likely to prove that the power of the state may be used to crush union-enforced colour bars. One can only hope that nationalistic fanaticism will not lead to gross injustices to the Whites. Kaunda and Nkumbula, the leaders of the present African coalition, have given assurances that they will not wish to dispense with the know-how and experience of the Whites. But they will have to compete with extremist rivals who have already thought it profitable to make rather reckless threats.

MINE OWNERS' EXPEDIENCY

Is there any sense in which the blame for the obvious injustices to Africans of the Mines and Works Act might be laid on the shoulders of the employers – the mining corporations? It could perhaps be held that corporation directorates and managements have been more concerned with the appeasement of their present staff – 'maintenance of good industrial relations' – than with the less easily envisaged interests of the community as consumers and the interests of the under-privileged classes. That is, directorates and managements may have failed in their duty to resist attempts by labour unions to enforce wage-rate increases which have priced much *potential* output beyond the reach of income,[1] thereby destroying employment opportunities for less fortunate persons, classes or races who have been striving to improve their material condition.

But is it not even more the duty of the state than it is of managements to resist any private coercion which frustrates the natural tendency of the market to break down customary and historical obstacles to equality of opportunity? And has it not in fact been legislation which has robbed the entrepreneurial classes of most of their power to act for the common interest? Not only has their effectiveness against labour union exploitation been gravely hindered, but their incentive to defend the community has been largely sapped.

If managements are blamed for colour injustices in South Africa, through weakly appeasing instead of resisting labour union pressures, we must remember, first, that they have equally been acting against the interests of the shareholders to whom they have been responsible; and, second, that public opinion, reinforced by professional moralists in pulpit, press and parliament, has not only condoned the private use of the coercive power of the strike but almost invariably praised arrangements under which corporations have agreed collusively to surrender to that coercion. Any action taken by the mines which would really have furthered the interests of the Africans would, indeed, have called forth the strongest condemnation from the growing 'progressive' opinion in Britain and the Western world generally.

---

[1] In the case of the gold mines, of course, the effect has been to reduce payable output without affecting the price.

Moreover, when the mining managements have thought in terms of cheapening output by offering opportunities for Africans to cheapen skills, in all probability they themselves have always felt an uneasy sense of guilt. Moral stereotypes have seemed therefore to coincide with expediency. In so far as the mines, by failing to fight labour union demands, have sacrificed the interests of their African employees and their shareholders, they have acquired the reputation of being 'generous employers' and of having served the cause of industrial peace!

The notion that low wage-rates for non-Whites enables the payment of higher wage-rates to Whites because employers can then 'afford' to pay them more, needs careful examination. It is true that in, say, mining, the source of the privileged earnings of the Whites would disappear if the cheap African labour ceased to be available, because the majority of the mines, if not all, would then have to close. It is equally true that the removal of colour bars in mining would slowly result in the ousting of certain categories of white employees from their present tasks. But this would greatly enhance the aggregate value of the product of mining. 'Employers' would be able to 'afford' to pay even more for white labour. Whether they could be forced to do so either through the market (competing demands for labour), through strike coercion or through legal edict is another matter.

The ratio system, under which a fixed numerical relationship between different categories of labour (defined by race or otherwise) with stipulated wage-rates is laid down,[1] cheapens the lower paid categories only by restricting demand for their services. In this sense alone may the better paid classes be said to be 'exploiting' the lower paid. Even so the ratio system has always been imposed (by the state or private coercion) on a free enterprise system. There is no inherent tendency for it to arise from within.

---

[1] This is now very common in South African industry as a result of the traditions established by the so-called 'civilised labour policy': see Chapter 8.

APPENDIX TO CHAPTER 7

COLLECTIVE BARGAINING AND THE NON-WHITES

IT MAY be felt that, although the power of the white labour unions was abused in the circumstances we have just discussed, collective bargaining remains essential to protect both Whites and non-Whites from exploitation. It is true that, in the extremely rare[1] cases in which managements are really in a position to exercise monopsonistic powers as 'monopoly' buyers of labour, 'exploitation' may occur. But in a good society, would not the prevention of this possibility be undertaken by the enforcement of laws designed to maintain competition and so prevent such abuses of managerial power? The need for this action by the state in a liberal society is first, to protect the right of the community as consumers to have access to the least-cost source of supply; and second, to protect the right of the community as entrepreneurs to substitute the least-cost form of output. It has been the denial of this second right which has created the grossest injustices to which, as producers – i.e., as wage-earners – the non-Whites have been subjected.

I cannot here attempt to explain the almost universal current tolerance of the private or sectional use of coercive power (or of state fixing of prices and wage-rates).[2] But the sceptical reader might give his mind to the following considerations.[3]

If the price of timber rises, the price of furniture will rise;

---

[1] The 'rare' is my own judgment after nearly four decades of interest in the question.

[2] It should be noticed that the case for such protection by the state does not justify resort to the fixing of prices of wage-rates by state edict, except in the case of 'natural monopolies'.

[3] The logic of this problem is discussed in my *Theory of Collective Bargaining* (1930, reprinted in 1954).

and if the price of the labour making the furniture rises, again the price of furniture will rise for exactly the same reason. The circumstances in which such a reaction would not follow are of negligible importance; yet most economists have obscured this vital issue by concentrating all attention upon the obviously unimportant theoretical case in which a rise in material prices or in wage-rates is absorbed to the detriment of profit claimants or interest claimants on the value of the product. But when the price of any commodity is raised above the free market level, by strike threat or action or by state edict, the effect is always regressive, harming poorer consumers relatively more than wealthier consumers. Moreover, such a process distorts investment in human capital. It causes, *inter alia*, relatively more people to be trained for and employed in occupations of low productivity and remuneration, and hence relatively few to be trained for and employed in occupations of high productivity and remuneration. And in South Africa it has been the non-Whites who have suffered most harm from this process. It has occurred most seriously (as we shall see) since the middle 1920s mainly through standard rate enforcement under the Industrial Conciliation Act and the Wage Act.

CHAPTER 8

THE 'CIVILISED LABOUR' ERA

DURING the First World War, the white miners' union[1] had succeeded in enforcing wage-rate increases many times larger than those obtained by the unorganised Africans. But the position of the latter had in some respects improved because, through the emergency, they had been permitted to undertake semi-skilled work especially as drill-sharpeners. This opportunity for a small proportion of Africans mitigated the increased costs of mining gold, the price of which rose to a premium after the war for a short period only. When it was obvious that the sterling price of gold would return to its standard level, the mine-owners naturally attempted to retain Africans in semi-skilled tasks and tried further to obtain some relaxation of other wasteful provisions enforced through regulations under the 1911 Colour Bar Act. They asked for a ratio of 10.5 Africans to 1 White; but the labour union demanded 3.5 to 1. A disastrous strike followed in 1922. The miners were supported by a general strike on the Rand,[2] which developed into virtually an armed uprising. Those who revolted were mainly Afrikaners, but as always the extremists of the Left were experts in the art of fishing in troubled waters. W. H. Andrews, who was shortly to become Secretary of the Communist Party in South Africa, played a leading role in this fight for white privilege. The revolt was crushed but powerful publicity had been given to the notion that the Whites were fighting against capitalist exploiters for the preservation of their traditional and rightful economic supremacy. In that sense, the strike, which has been called the 'colour bar strike', was a victory for Andrews and those who called themselves socialists.

At the time of the strike, the overwhelming majority of the white miners (foremen or artisans, as distinct from

---

[1] The South African Industrial Federation.
[2] The IWW pattern is again obvious.

executives) were Afrikaners from the Transvaal and the Orange Free State, and their anti-colour indoctrination had been fruitfully exploited from the first by the Marxist-indoctrinated inspirers and leaders of the insurrection, such as Andrews. The result was a great boost to the South African Labour Party, which was modelled more or less on its British counterpart and was on the best terms with the British trade-union movement. In 1924, largely through the impact upon White opinion of the 1922 strike, it obtained the chance of sharing in government through a coalition formed with the Nationalist Party, a socialistically-orientated party[1] representing Afrikaners who accepted the principle of White supremacy and non-White subjection. Without this active co-operation of a typically British sort of Socialist party to form a Labour-Nationalist 'Pact', the era which introduced the most serious forms of colour injustice might never have emerged.

Although Labour politicians may be accused of sacrificing their ideals in the lust for office and the unions of perverting the movement to racist ends, they were enthusiastically supported by the great majority of the adherents of the Labour Party. Moreover, the laws they used most successfully to keep the non-Whites in economic inferiority were of a kind which, as I shall be showing, are praised by collectivist thinking everywhere.

THE MINES AND WORKS ACT, 1926

The Nationalist-Labour 'Pact' Government introduced early the second 'Colour Bar Act' – the Mines and Works Act of 1926 – to satisfy the demands of the 1922 strikers. This was probably the most honest and most drastic piece of colour bar legislation which the world has ever experienced, just as the 'civilised labour policy' – which they inaugurated immediately on attaining power – was probably the most dishonest and yet most effective plan for enforcing a colour bar the world has ever experienced.

It is unnecessary to discuss the details of the Mines and Works Act of 1926. In brief, it established the legality of the colour bars imposed by regulations under the 1911 Act.

---

[1]See Chapter 5, pp. 43-4.

These regulations had been challenged in the Courts so as to render the position obscure, and the effect of the Act was to entrench more unequivocally the barriers against African advancement.

But in spite of this open perpetuation of exclusiveness it was, in my judgment, a less serious barrier to the non-Whites than those introduced through the fine sounding 'civilised labour policy'. Worked out jointly by the (mainly Afrikaans-speaking) Nationalists and the (mainly English-speaking) Socialists, this policy was represented as an attempt to protect 'civilised' or 'European' standards. It differed from the Mines and Works Act in that it imposed no overt colour bar and could therefore be approved by those who felt that Socialism implies some sort of equality. Yet, above all, its protagonists could argue that their object was solely to preserve a tolerable standard of living, 'from the usual European standpoint', for all who had achieved a civilised way of life, no matter what their colour.

AIMS OF THE 'CIVILISED LABOUR POLICY'

Now if the preservation of existing standards had been genuinely the aim, it would have represented an objective which I myself have always actively and explicity advocated. No one has insisted more strongly than I on the importance of honouring 'established expectations' in a good society;[1] provided that this does not create a permanent barrier to equality of opportunity.

Had the aim gone no further than ensuring that the average absolute standards of the Whites then living did not decline – that is, if the object had been that of preventing any 'levelling down' whilst permitting a 'levelling up'—there would have been much to be said for it. The growth of the national income by allowing the entry of the non-Whites into better remunerated and more productive industrial

---

[1] For instance, this principle of honouring 'established expectations' formed a major thesis in *Plan for Reconstruction*, published in 1943. I argued that, in the dissolution of economic privileges in countries of homogeneous population like the United Kingdom, it was essential to do so in such a manner that the privileges were dissolved gradually, because innocent people had planned or adjusted their lives to a society in which these privileges existed. See also *Economists and the Public* (1936), Chapter XXI.

employments would then have raised non-white standards relatively to those of Whites. But state intervention was used not simply to prevent a fall in the standards of the Whites. It was used also to ensure the maintenance of *relative* white standards – an insistence upon special privilege of the kind that labour unions everywhere frequently defend as 'differentials'. Consequently there has been far less 'levelling up' since 1924 (in spite of an enormous increase in real national income) than the unhampered market would have achieved. The failure of non-Whites to share more liberally in this internal progress constitutes the major source of colour injustice in all its forms.[1]

The 'civilised labour policy' was shrewdly built on a recognition of the following realities:

(a) that there already existed a powerful prejudice on the part of white employees against working side by side with Coloureds or Africans unless the latter were subordinates;

(b) that the educational facilities and sociological background of the non-Whites were markedly inferior;[2]

(c) that insistence on the standard rate could, in the light of the above factors, effectively but unobtrusively keep the non-Whites out of the Whites' preserves – an insight which led the Labour Party to make 'the rate for the job' the foundation of the new policy;

(d) that recourse to the apprenticeship system would not only exclude the majority of non-Whites from qualification in the trades covered, because few could attain the educational standard laid down, but also exclude this few by reason of the composition of the boards of selection;

(e) that employers' representatives on the apprenticeship

---

[1] For if the earnings and living standards of the Coloureds, Indians and Africans had risen more rapidly, it would have been easier for them to achieve greater equality of respect (see Chapter 3, p. 29) and increasingly difficult to withhold from them a more appropriate share in political power.

[2] These initial disadvantages have been partly due to over-indulgence by many in cheap liquor and even the use of an easily (though illegally) obtainable drug known as 'dagga'. But already rising industrial opportunities have been accompanied by a marked improvement in habits and behaviour.

boards would be led by their natural wish for collaboration with the labour representatives in excluding from skilled operations such non-Whites (chiefly Coloured) as were able to acquire the legally enacted educational grades;

(f) that even where educational and sociological factors and the prejudices of white employees were not powerful hindrances to the profitable employment of non-Whites, the insistence (under the Factories Act) upon separate facilities would often make their employment impossibly expensive in established industries;

(g) that the labour union movement was already operating on the principle of the 'closed shop';

(h) that the application of this principle would reinforce the other devices which were excluding non-Whites from the better paid employments.

THE 'RATE FOR THE JOB'

The 'rate for the job' was the vital principle in the most powerful yet most subtle colour bar that has ever operated. Equal pay for equal work (i.e., for identical outputs of a given quality) is a result of the neutrality of the free non-discriminatory market. It is no method of achieving such a market. When the standard wage-rate is forced above the free market level (whether through legal enactment or the strike threat), thereby reducing the output which can be produced profitably, it must have the effect of preventing the entry of subordinate races or classes into the protected field or of actually excluding them from it.[1] This has been by far the most effective method of preserving white privileges, largely because it can be represented as non-discriminatory. Whereas some of the policies of the Labour-Nationalist Pact amounted to blatant discrimination (such as the deliberate dismissal of non-Whites in order to employ Whites in government service), the effects of the 'civilised labour' restraints have been far more important. They have

---

[1] The gradual complete exclusion, by means of the standard rate, of women compositors (type-setters) who at one time were widely employed in that craft in Britain, is an interesting illustration. See S. and B. Webb, *Industrial Democracy*, pp. 488, 500, 504-5.

rendered much more formidable those restraints imposed by custom and prejudice that have debarred non-Whites from avenues of economic advancement. They have, indeed, had a more unjust impact than 'influx control' and 'job reservation' under *apartheid*.

The group that has suffered most by the barring of non-Whites from the better economic opportunities has been the Coloured people, who make up about one-tenth of the total population of the Republic. In an article I published in 1938 I referred to certain aspects of the 'civilised labour policy' as 'an insuperable obstacle to the achievement of Coloured aspirations'. But although this assertion remains true,[1] I had not perceived in 1937 the extent to which entrepreneurial ingenuity was then surmounting some of the obstacles and, through providing better opportunities for the Coloureds and Africans, permitting the standards of all races to rise.[2]

In spite of the economic injustices suffered by the Coloured people, they have little right to moral indignation against their white comrades, because they themselves have likewise sought to exclude the competition of Africans who have enjoyed even less privilege and power than themselves.[3] Their feelings are perfectly natural. Did not Josiah Tucker remark, in the 18th century, that 'all men would be monopolists if they could.' We are here concerned, however, not with the human failings which have led to race injustices but with the types of social organisation which permit and buttress these injustices. The lesson of history, explained by classical economic analysis, is that disinterested market pressures, under the profit-seeking inducement, provide the only objective, systematic discipline that would dissolve traditional barriers and offer opportunities irrespective of race or colour.

---

[1] For instance, in 1960–61 less than a thousand Coloureds were indentured in the Western Cape out of a total of over 13,000. Yet last century there had been more Coloured than White artisans in the Cape. Coloured apprentices are now confined almost entirely to building and furniture. If a trend started recently under 'job reservation' continues, they may be gradually ousted from the building industry. (See Chapter 13, p. 118.)
[2] See Chapter 9.
[3] See below, pp. 77–8, and Chapter 17, p. 172.

COLOUR BAR LEGISLATION

I shall make no attempt to give a comprehensive and balanced summary of the legislation through which the 'civilised labour policy' was enacted; for I shall be concerned solely with its relationship to 'injustice', real or imagined, between one race or colour and another.

This policy relied upon the Factories Act of 1918, the Apprenticeship Act of 1922 and the Industrial Conciliation Act of 1924, which preceded the Nationalist-Labour Pact. The new policy aimed at reinforcing the powers of discrimination which were latent in the former Acts.

Much of the content of the Factories Act (of 1918) satisfied the 'liberal' criterion of serving the collective (as distinct from the sectional) interest. But it was an example of discriminatory state intervention in so far as it conferred arbitrary power on the Minister of Labour to withdraw some exemptions from customs-duties on raw materials. Exemption could be withdrawn if, in the Minister's opinion, 'satisfactory labour conditions' were not being maintained; and factory inspectors under the Department of Labour made it clear that 'unsatisfactory' was interpreted to mean employing non-Whites when Whites were available. The Act required also that there should be separate facilities for the white and non-white races in such things as toilets, rest-rooms, canteens, etc., and although the original purpose was separation rather than economic discrimination, the architects of the 'civilised labour policy' perceived full well that the increased costs of employing non-Whites in firms in which they had not previously been employed, combined with other legislative provisions, would have the effect of excluding many of them from industrial employment.

The Apprenticeship Act (of 1922) was genuinely believed by many, including some well-meaning educationists who helped draft it, to have had the purpose of encouraging white youths to acquire industrial skills. In practice, the Act has probably had the opposite effect. Certainly, administered in the spirit of the 'civilised labour policy', it has assisted in reserving the better-remunerated employments for the Whites, but in such a way that it has weakened the incentive for self-improvement among them. Thus, whilst it developed facilities for training in technical colleges and made attendance compulsory for apprentices, it never insisted upon them passing the examinations in order to qualify. Consequently, the majority have never treated seriously the expensive facilities provided; they become journeymen merely by the passage of time. The only material amendment in this respect, introduced in 1963, has the effect of delaying by one year the period of qualification of apprentices who do not pass the examinations, although whilst waiting passively for qualifications they will be paid 70 per cent of the journeyman's wage, a policy the Minister of Labour described as 'tough'.

The Wage Act of 1925 was aimed at easing the Poor White problem and preserving white civilisation by restricting competition from non-Whites. It did so through applying the principle of the standard rate to spheres of employment where no labour unions had then been formed – the very avenues through which the entrepreneurial search for cheap labour was tending most directly to raise relative non-white standards. The wording of the original Wage Act was explicit in excluding discrimination on grounds of race or colour, but its sponsors made it quite obvious that they were trying to protect the higher civilisation from the competition of the lower civilisation, and dragged in such red herrings as the prevention of 'sweating', and the need to encourage efficiency by higher earnings. Subsequent amendments, however, made the discriminatory objective more explicit. The Wage Board concentrated, for many years after its establishment under the Act, upon employments where Whites were in actual or potential competition with the Coloureds or Indians. That is, they did not bother about the remuneration of work performed by non-Whites in which there was virtually no competition with Whites. With few exceptions, it was only after the amendment of the Act in 1937 that typically Coloured spheres of employment were directly covered.

Whatever the original intentions, the Act has come to serve as a protection not only of relatively unskilled white labour against non-Whites, but (since 1937) of Coloured and Asiatics against the Africans; for the industrial boom caused by the quiet speeding up of racial economic integration in the 1930s created rapidly growing opportunities of industrial employment, first for Coloured women and later for Coloured men and Indians.[1] Today the majority of those covered by the Act are the non-Whites other than Africans, and it has protected the former at the expense of slowing down the rate of progress of the latter.[2]

Under the Industrial Conciliation Act (of 1924) industrial councils are established, made up of representatives of employers' associations and of labour unions. Together they negotiate wage-rates, hours of labour and fringe benefits. Any agreement may then obtain (and in practice almost automatically obtains) approval of the Minister of Labour. It then has the force of law; and the Minister may order its provisions to apply to employers and employees in the same or cognate industries who have not been parties to the agreement, in any areas, at his discretion. During the period of such agreements, strikes or lock-outs about matters which the industrial councils have determined are illegal; and for other matters of dispute there are provisions, similar to those common elsewhere, for conciliation and arbitration. White, Coloured and Indian ('Asiatic') employees are covered by the Act but Africans are excluded. Broadly speaking, Africans have no rights under it.

This Act appeared superficially to have as its principal objective the laudable aim of preventing further outbreaks of violence such as occurred during the 1922 strike. Since its passage, South Africa has experienced an industrial peace many other countries might envy. But this success has been because, since 1924, the political power of the Whites has been used to secure the subservience of the non-Whites without strike action. The superficial effect of the Act has been to reduce the power of the labour unions and the relative absence of strikes may suggest that members have become apathetic and that officials have lost their militancy. This, however, is an illusion. Through the virtually automatic conferring of the force of law upon agreements reached, the effective ability of the unions to protect

---

[1] Indian women were, by a strong tradition of their own race, for some time excluded from the opportunities which would otherwise have been open to them. They are now beginning to accept employment in industry.

[2] See above, p.73.

the privileges of their members has been magnified.

The associated managements have combined with the labour representatives to create a joint monopoly under which the two parties provide mutual protection for one another against competition.[1] This protection can ultimately be effected only through the exclusion of labour and other resources from employment where their contributions to the community's real income could have been largest. Yet it seems directly to benefit the joint monopolists. For instance, it makes things easy for managements in 'maintaining good industrial relations'; and because all firms represented agree to the same wage-rates and conditions, there is no increase in the competitive burden of costs.

Such complacency is, however, based on a static view of the economic process. The 'employers' representatives' who have accepted the system have failed to realise that the demand for the product of any one industry is a function of non-competing output; in other words, since all industries are covered by one or other form of wage legislation, they have all been restricting the real demand for one another's products. The tempo of development has been much slower than would have resulted from the raising of aggregate industrial earnings through the employment of larger numbers of non-Whites.

Originally, the Act was effective in protecting the Whites at the expense of opportunities of advancement for Coloureds and Indians. It seemed to be unnecessary to worry about competition with Africans in the industries in which labour was organised until the 1930s, when already there were signs of extensive entrepreneurial circumvention of the 'civilised labour policy'. In 1930 it was deemed expedient to include an amendment to ensure that, in those very rare instances where Africans came to be employed in any type of work to which an industrial council agreement applied, they should be paid the agreed remuneration and receive the agreed benefits. If the African leaders had understood the working of the economic system, they would have seen in this condition not a right but an injustice to their people.

The Industrial Conciliation Act appears, on the whole,

---

[1] See my *Theory of Collective Bargaining*, pp. 133 *et seq.*

to have favoured the Whites in a grossly unfair manner, especially in occupations dominated by the Whites when it was passed in the early 1920s. But it would be wrong to suppose that all industrial councils have represented white employees alone, or have been dominated by them. In the new industries such as clothing which emerged in the 1930s (through entrepreneurial avoidance of the spirit and aims of the 'civilised labour policy'), the Coloured employees came to be strongly represented; and in industries where the labour unions are dominated by Coloureds, the incentive to bring Africans into semi-skilled occupations seems to have been weakened.[1] On the other hand, the organisation of the Coloureds through industrial councils may have had the effect (before job reservation in 1956 and 1959) of protecting them not only against the potential competition of Africans but also against moves to oust them from their existing channels of employment for the benefit of Whites.[2]

EFFECTS ON EMPLOYMENT, EFFICIENCY AND TRAINING

Returning now to the 'civilised labour policy' as a whole, we can see that because the methods adopted were not fully understood, some of the classes intended to benefit were sometimes harmed. In the years immediately following its introduction the direct beneficiaries were the established white artisan classes, whilst the minimum wage and apprenticeship legislation excluded not only poorer non-Whites from contributing more to the common pool of output but also the Poor Whites (mainly Afrikaners). The latter, also, were prevented from discounting their initial inferiority in literacy and general adaptation to urban pursuits. Indeed, as I have pointed out, the Poor White problem was 'solved' only when entrepreneurial ingenuities, stimulated by world events which enhanced prospective profits from the more productive use of labour resources, succeeded in avoiding the intentions of legislation and bringing about a measure of racial integration in industry.

It goes without saying that all these restrictions on the market determination of the form of employment and re-

---

[1] The Coloured labour unions have tended to be dominated by leaders from the extreme Left.
[2] See Chapter 11, pp. 105-6.

muneration have depressed labour efficiency as a whole. 'Civilised labour' restraints have forced the employment of unsuitable people in the protected fields. They have entailed an enormous waste of potential talent of the non-Whites. They have caused the overcrowding and unjust cheapening of the occupations to which the non-Whites have been confined. They have vitiated the efficiency of the non-Whites by destroying incentives for self-improvement and training under 'the rate for the job'. And they have weakened incentives to efficiency on the part of the Whites who have been feather-bedded.

By comparison, the initial disadvantages of the non-Whites due to home background and lack of resources for investment in their own education have in themselves been a minor hindrance to their progress. It will generally pay private enterprise to see that education, both general and technical, is made available where openings for the employment of the attributes and skills acquired are not likely to be suppressed.[1] But powerful custom or prejudice, collusive action and legal enactment, by closing potential avenues of employment may destroy the motive for investment in human capital. Indeed, it will be wasteful for the state, for business concerns or for parents to devote resources to training and equally pointless for individuals to devote their energies and limited incomes to such purposes. But there would have been an irresistibly strong demand for developing the industrial usefulness of the Coloureds if it had not been for fears that any such move would have encountered other legislative steps to render unusable the skills so developed. The profit motive is powerful; but when it is likely to be overruled by legislation or regulation its power to serve the community is hamstrung.

EFFECT OF LEGISLATION ON AFRICANS

We must briefly refer in this context to the effects upon the Africans. About the time that the Wage Act was passed, the Economic and Wage Commission of 1925 forecast that the consequence of standard rate enforcement was likely to be the exclusion of Africans. It had indeed been the hope of

---

[1] I am not suggesting that it is not an appropriate function of the state to finance education, both general and technical.

the Labour Party that, through the Wage Act and the Industrial Conciliation Act, African labour could be kept permanently out of the industrial system. This time the force of profit-seeking incentives proved more powerful than legislation, and (as we shall see) the attempt to segregate the Africans from the modern world and confine them to primitive tribalism in the reserves, or to labouring work on the farms and mines, was far from successful. It barred them only from semi-skilled and skilled employments and not from work classed as unskilled.

Of course, there were sincere supporters of the 'civilised labour policy' who believed it would truly raise the Coloureds and Africans to the white man's standards,[1] and equally sincere opponents who objected to it for precisely this reason. Thus, some of the most effective parliamentary criticism of the Wage Act (from the parliamentary Opposition – then the 'South African Party') arose from the belief that it would have its claimed effects and raise the earnings of the non-Whites, thus disturbing the existing non-white subservience. Other Opposition members believed (equally fallaciously) that employers could afford to pay high wage-rates to Whites because of the economies achieved in paying low wage-rates to non-Whites; and they opposed the Wage Act because they thought it might be used to raise Coloured and African wage-rates and hence ultimately reduce the earnings of Whites.

The 'civilised labour policy' was not more sharply criticised abroad because it was in full concord with developments that were coming to be welcomed by well-meaning idealists in all countries. In most countries governments were seeking, under pressures through the voting system, directly or indirectly, permanently to enrich political majorities at the expense of political minorities. They believed that it was possible, through the fixing of standard wage-rates, to transfer income permanently from investors as a whole to employees as a whole; and many believed, falsely but sincerely, that this would bring about a permanent transfer of income from rich to poor.

---

[1] In part this idea was based on the fallacy that rapacious employers could exploit the non-Whites because their 'needs' were less than those of the Whites.

Through the stereotypes so formed, such feelings of economic injustice as exist in South Africa tend to be directed not only against the law and administration which have openly or deviously denied opportunities to those of the wrong skin pigmentation, but also against the abstraction called 'capitalism'. Thus indignation and resentments are apt to be aimed against the very forces that have, in themselves, exerted the only effective pressures towards the economic uplift of the underprivileged races. For political action by the Coloureds and Africans has been wholly impotent, whereas entrepreneurs have (as we shall see in the following Chapter) often been shrewd enough to find ways of surmounting the chief barriers (i.e., the Wage Act, the Industrial Conciliation Act and the Apprenticeship Act). Despite being allowed relatively little scope, the profit incentive has been the chief source of the dissolution of colour injustices and hence must be accorded the main credit for the remarkable rise in South Africa's national income since the 1930s. The non-Whites have nearly all shared in the benefits – the Africans (largely because they had no effective labour unions) proportionately more than any other group (see Table below) until 'economic planning' in the form of 'influx control' (discussed in Chapter 15) began, after the Second World War, to exclude them from opportunities which would normally have been available.

PROPORTION OF AGGREGATE SALARIES AND WAGES PAID TO EACH RACE IN PRIVATE INDUSTRY IN THE REPUBLIC OF SOUTH AFRICA[1]

Year	Whites	Africans	Indians	Coloureds
1932–3	73.6	15.2	2.5	8.7
1939–40	71.7	18.0	2.5	8.8
1946–7	62.2	24.6	2.8	10.4
1956–7	61.8	25.0	3.1	10.1
1960–1	61.5	25.2		13.3

[1]This Table may, unless qualified, leave a wrong impression. Average earnings (salaries and wages) per head of Africans, as a proportion of the average earnings of Whites, rose steadily from 12% in 1933–4 to 24.7% in 1946–7. After that year, mainly because of "influx control", a bigger proportion of Africans than the free market would have determined, found employment in less productive and less well paid areas. Hence, the percentage of African to white earnings per head fell steadily to 18% in 1958–9. Since then it has recovered to 18.5% in 1960–1.

CHAPTER 9

RACIAL INTEGRATION AND INDUSTRIAL GROWTH

ALTHOUGH the 'civilised labour' legislation had erected the most formidable barriers to non-white advancement in the industrial sphere, the profit urge – coupled with entrepreneurial ingenuity – still disclosed ways round some of the barriers. The result was to bring about, from the middle 1930s, significant changes in the racial composition of the industrial labour force. Two important stimuli enhanced prospective yields and hence the free market incentives for the avoidance of colour bar obstacles.

The first was the 1934 rise in the dollar price of gold, which enormously increased the ability of South African secondary industries to compete successfully against the rest of the world for her own and imported raw materials. The second was the need to offset the labour shortage caused by the Second World War.

Encouraged by the increased gold price, investors sought out new fields of industrial employment (such as the clothing industry) which had not been monopolised by white labour unions. To obtain labour cheap enough to permit the product of this employment to be priced for mass consumption, managements began, broadly speaking, by successfully competing with the occupations of housewife or domestic servant and attracting first white women and then Coloured women into the new factories. The resulting expansion of real income caused a general expansion of demand for the product of all industries, which made it possible for many Coloured employees who had been working as mere labourers to progress by stepping into jobs from which Whites had been promoted, whilst Africans took over the jobs from which the Coloureds were promoted. The fact that the Coloured people had, despite the Wage Act, relatively little power[1] to protect themselves against the competition of the relatively very much poorer African labourers undoubtedly worked to their collective benefit, since the rapid increase in the number of Africans in factory employments, by making industrial growth profitable, multiplied openings for Coloured women as well as men.

The Second World War enhanced the stimulus. The impetus to economic development which has so often occurred in wartime has puzzled some economists. In spite of the destruction and patent waste of resources in war, the real income of a nation has often been larger at the end than at the beginning of the conflict. One reason is that the emergency forces the abandonment of scarcity-creating practices by such policies as 'dilution' which overcome restraints on labour utilisation and reduce the valuation of leisure (and of services such as those of the housewife). In South Africa after 1939, not only were non-Whites admitted to better-paid (and hence more productive) kinds of industrial employment in private industry, but even in government activities they were permitted to take on many jobs previously performed by Whites.

EVASION OF 'CIVILISED LABOUR POLICY'

The avoidance of the 'civilised labour policy' through these developments was accompanied, since 1933[2], by some measure of actual evasion, particularly in the smaller factories. By 'evasion' I mean that some 'unqualified' Coloureds and even Africans managed to find skilled or responsible employment without apprenticeship.

The sociological effects over the space of three decades have been far-reaching. The Coloureds have become incomparably better dressed, better fed, better housed, better behaved, more literate, more efficient, more articulate and more resentful. Indeed, following the quiet circumvention from 1933 onwards of the restrictive laws of the middle

---

[1] See Chapter 8, p. 73.
[2] A new coalition government acquired power in 1933. It merged into one 'United Party', the former Opposition Party (the South African Party), some Nationalists and some Labour Party members. Fortunately, the Labour representatives seem to have failed to perceive what was happening.

1920s, a social revolution has occurred among the urban Coloured people – a change expressed in the most striking manner in the achievement of a large measure of 'equality of aspect'. Within the space of a decade or so, Coloured women, formerly drably or poorly dressed on the whole, have become pleasingly, neatly and even fashionably dressed. With Coloured men, who still mostly perform various kinds of unskilled or rough manual work, this revolution in dress and aspect has been rather less obvious.[1] But the general appearance, as well as the health, of this group has improved remarkably since entrepreneurial enterprise, under the stimulation of the 'profit motive', succeeded in dodging the state-imposed barriers. Increased income made possible other forms of social progress unimagined three decades ago. For example, the phenomenally successful 'Eoan Group', a multi-racial but mainly Coloured organisation, has produced excellent operas,[2] ballets,[2] musical comedies, plays, oratorios, etc. And non-white participation in sport (officially segregated)[3] has increased rapidly although facilities are still markedly inferior. All these developments have created a growing feeling of respect for the urban Coloured communities and, what is even more important, growing self-respect among them.

The revolution in aspect, the astonishing improvement in the general standard of dress, coupled with improved health from childhood, seems to have caused Coloured women to grow in attractiveness for white men. It has, I believe, provided an important motivation for the Immorality Act (which forbids sexual relations, within marriage or otherwise, between Whites and non-Whites), whilst the con-

---

[1] The change was facilitated because the Coloured women largely worked in the new clothing factories from which they could buy cheaply. The progress of Coloured women preceded that of Coloured men, creating some curious sociological problems in the middle 1930s, when Coloured women were often earning more than their husbands.

[2] Due credit should be given to the College of Music and the Ballet School of the University of Cape Town for these achievements.

[3] Unpublicised sporting events involving participants of more than one racial group have been increasing. Such activities have not yet been declared illegal. The excellent achievements of non-Whites in the sporting sphere have increased considerably the respect in which they are held.

tinued economic progress of Coloured men and women has, I feel, been one of the main motivations also for the 'job reservation policy' and labour direction on the Communist model inaugurated in 1955.[1]

ENTERPRISE AND LIVING STANDARDS

But the whole prosperity and economic expansion of South Africa has been due to the use of non-white labour in occupations and grades of work which would have been prevented for all time if the restrictionist-minded Labour Party members of the 'Pact' Government of 1924 had had their way. That is, the rapidly improving material standards of all classes since the middle 1930s, but particularly of the Poor Whites, the Coloureds, the Indians, and (above all) the Africans, were the consequence, wholly and entirely, of profit-seeking enterprise and ingenuity, factors which were obstructed in every possible direction by state action to protect the earnings of favoured races or groups against capitalists' attempts to purchase labour at wage-rates which consumers could afford.

If the intentions of the Labour-Nationalist coalition had not been circumvented, if entrepreneurial ingenuities had not by-passed restraints on the profit system, the poorer Afrikaners would have been forced to acquiesce much longer in their economically and socially backward state of the late 1920s. Not realising the sacrifice they were making, they might then have been prepared to shoulder the burden of 'separate development', which they are definitely not prepared to do today. It may indeed have been practicable, until the 1930s, to dispense with African labour entirely, except on the mines and on the farms, where the Africans had already become indispensable. The cost would have been the acceptance of more or less permanent Poor Whiteism.[2] But the consequent persistence of urban impoverishment among the Whites and the Coloured people

---

[1] See Chapter 15.
[2] It is difficult to conceive of any form of technological progress which could have compensated for the loss of the Africans' contribution to the dynamics of expansion (in the form of an accelerating increase in the supply of industrial labour) since 1930.

would then have made it easier to blame the avarice of 'profit-seeking employers'; whilst the Africans, excluded from industrial opportunities, would have been aware of fewer grievances than they now believe they have against the Whites and, mistakenly, against the 'capitalist system'.

CHAPTER 10

AFRICANS IN THE TOWNS

WE HAVE seen that the solution of the Poor White problem (and incidentally the partial solution of the problem of the Poor Coloureds) required not only the more productive use of non-white labour generally but the settlement of Africans in or on the borders of towns, as a cheap source of 'put and carry' labour. This alone permitted the new products of economic integration to be profitable, i.e., capable of being priced within reach of the community's income.

THE URBANISATION OF THE AFRICAN
The sizeable influx of Africans to the towns (as distinct from the mining compounds) began shortly after the First World War, and was remarkably accelerated in the middle 1930s. It seemed to create the problem of the Poor Black. In reality it merely focused attention on it, since conditions that appear tolerable in tribal areas or on farms become intolerable in the relatively advanced sociological environment of modern industrial towns.[1] Hence, when the number of urban Africans began growing rapidly, the need to redress the difficulties created by their primitive standards and customs became urgent.

When Africans first enter secondary industrial employments and other town occupations, they are usually quite unprepared for urban life. They find themselves in a bewildering environment where their tribal traditions, whilst still powerful, retain little meaning; they are submerged in a community whose language the majority do not at first understand; they are mostly housed in barracks – isolated from their wives and children; and they are engaged in serving a society which makes it clear to them that they are not regarded as eventual citizens but rather as permanent foreigners or (more recently) as temporary foreign visitors.

[1] See Chapter 4, p. 32.

The most tenaciously rooted tribal traditions lose some of their hold with urban contacts, even with such restricted contacts as are permitted under the compound system. It is generally agreed that, after about a decade devoted to town employments, significant psycho-sociological changes occur. Some believe that Africans of the second generation in the towns are already essentially detribalised or urbanised, their links with the reserves having been irretrievably weakened. But although only a very small proportion of urban Africans have been born in the towns (probably not more than 2 per cent), growing numbers have now been town dwellers for two, three or four generations. These are increasingly referred to as 'rootless'; their literacy is growing;[1] they have ceased to be pagan in the usual sense of the word; their belief in witchcraft is losing its hold; they are learning to respect and place their trust in modern medicine (including patent medicines); they attach themselves readily to those Christian churches (including Christian sects they themselves have originated) which are willing to accept and respect them; but they have not thrown off all tribal superstitions and practices, especially the powerful tradition of lobola, a form of wife purchase (even when they have been married according to Christian as distinct from pagan rites).[2] Growing numbers of urban Africans have been falling into this mainly, although not perfectly, detribalised class. That they feel perplexed, adrift, *désorientés*, is only to be expected.

URBAN ADAPTATION AND THE 'PASS LAWS'
The disintegration of the stable sociological attitudes of the tribal social structure, accompanied by an imperfect adaptation of the African's attitudes towards the urban environment, would have created major tensions under the most enlightened government. Instead, the strains have been enormously aggravated by 'influx control' and the manner in which the pass system has been administered.

---

[1] It has been estimated that in the Cape Town area less than 30 per cent of employed Africans are illiterate, although about a quarter are literate in the Xhosa language only.
[2] This is probably the case with approximately half the Africans in urban areas other than mining areas.

Nevertheless, although Africans seem often to be miserably unhappy during the long periods of adjustment, their material advancement in urban employment is such that hardly any ever wish to return permanently to the reserves, or to the mines or the farms. Of course, unless their wives and families have been allowed to live with them as urban dwellers, they nearly all look forward to retiring to the reserves. Perhaps between one-fifth and one-quarter now regard the urban areas as their homes. A surprisingly high proportion of Africans employed in industry seems to have been attracted from employment in the mines, which first persuaded them to leave the reserves. Their real earnings as unskilled labourers in industry and commerce, although considerably lower than of Whites with equal muscular strength and intelligence, are high in relation to what they can command in other spheres.

Since they first came to the towns, Africans have been able to satisfy demand for their traditional food, clothing and shelter by the expenditure of a relatively small proportion of their current earnings. Some of their wages are (usually) sent to their families and dependents in the reserves.[1] The balance they have gradually come to use in acquiring 'luxuries' in the form of what we regard as the 'conventional necessities' of the Whites. In earlier years, many Africans regarded money income earned outside the reserves chiefly as a source of acquiring additional cattle,[2] but they have usually taken easily to the sort of status-conferring goods which the white man conspicuously possesses: smart suits, hats and footwear; blankets, mattresses and bedsteads; crockery and kitchen utensils; sewing machines; clocks and watches; radios; gramophones and musical instruments; bicycles and even cars;[3] patent medicines; tea and processed foods; alcoholic liquor (until recently, illegally purchased); insurance and investment in savings

---

[1] The growing population of the reserves, itself a response to enhanced urban earnings (in the mines and elsewhere), could not now subsist without contributions from African earnings outside.
[2] The possession of cattle confers prestige in the tribe. The traditional form of bride purchase is the transfer of cattle.
[3] It has been claimed recently that the *per capita* ownership of cars by Africans in the Republic is larger than that in Russia.

accounts; expenditure on sports as participants and spectators; betting and other forms of gambling. Although some of these things have replaced similar commodities provided by primitive native crafts, the availability of new products and forms of expenditure has inexorably diverted the course of tribal change in the direction of Western civilisation.

The most important expression of their 'luxury' demand has been, however, for 'leisure' in a special sense. Africans in urban employments (as in mining) have always temporarily saved a large part of their earnings, not as provision for old age or contingencies, but to pay for periodic visits to their families and friends in the reserves.[1] This has been largely, though not entirely, responsible for the high labour turnover of Africans in industrial and commercial employment.[2] The tradition has survived partly because it has been difficult (and is becoming virtually impossible) for Africans to bring their women-folk to the towns.[3] Moreover, some Africans return at the appropriate seasons to help with ploughing or harvesting.

It hardly needs stressing that the long recurrent periods of separation from their women-folk and families under this migrant labour system has created serious moral and sociological tensions among urban Africans, as well as among their children, who need the guidance of the head of the family.[4] Recent legislation (discussed in Chapter 15) is aggravating – at least temporarily – this situation, which is believed by some students to be a chief cause of the violent (but probably ephemeral) Poqo movement.[5] At the same

---

[1] Tribal Africans tend to be improvident in other senses; but as they become adjusted to urban life, they are capable of learning the meaning of thrift.

[2] African labour turnover is said to be much higher in these pursuits than in the mines. But Dr S. van der Horst has estimated that, in the Cape Town area, Africans over the age of 18 spend about 60 per cent of their working days in employment.

[3] The relative number of African women in urban areas seemed to have been increasing until the deliberate reversal of this trend during the last few years.

[4] Yet the original legislation which encouraged the perpetuation of this tradition aimed, at least ostensibly, at preventing social evils.

[5] Enquiries into recent riots brought out the fact that the rioters were wholly from single quarters. It has been reported that, at the Langa Location near Cape Town, 12,000 married Africans are living as bachelors in single quarters.

time, the majority of the Africans themselves seem to have no general wish to settle permanently in urban areas. They are reluctant to break contact with their people, and even children who are born in the towns are often sent to the reserves for upbringing and education, partly because it is cheaper but partly because the parents believe the environment is better.

ATTITUDE OF THE EMPLOYERS

When we deplore the results of large numbers of married men living in single quarters, we must remind ourselves that it was not market forces or profit-seeking incentives which entrenched the migratory system. In the early days, this system suited not only the needs of the mines but also the convenience of the Africans, who could easily spend short periods away from the reserves without disturbing their traditional mode of living. But whatever pragmatic factors were responsible for the inauguration of the migrant labour system, it was perpetuated by legislation.

Certainly managements (including those of the mines)[1] may be blamed for conforming too complacently to governmental policy and white public opinion. They have, perhaps, made too little effort to foster the detribalisation process. Yet they would always have welcomed a settled African labour force, with the stability and reduced labour turnover among their employees that a normal family life could be expected to create. Even last century the wiser leaders in the mining industry could see the advantages which would accrue if the Africans had been permitted to become permanent urban dwellers, together with their families.[2] For instance, the mines' recruitment organisation became adapted with a view to mitigating the burden and inconvenience of the continuous labour turnover for which the constant movement of Africans backwards and forwards was responsible.[3] Nevertheless the mine-owners – like the in-

---

[1] The problems of migratory African labour in the gold mines are complicated by the fact that about two-thirds of the Africans employed are foreigners. (See below, pp. 92-3, 99-100, and Chapter 17, p. 155.)
[2] See, for example, Doxey, *op. cit.*, p. 92.
[3] In recruiting Africans for mining work, their fares are frequently advanced. The usual contract is for periods of service of about nine months upwards, although the average is about 14 months. The Tomlin-

dustrialists of today – felt constrained rather to adjust their policy to the system than to attempt to fight it.

An experiment in the gold-mining industry serves to highlight the manner in which market forces have tended, in themselves, to encourage the emergence of settled labour forces, and permit even Africans employed in mines to enjoy a normal family life, whilst the power of the state has been used in the opposite way, to prevent such a development. Little more than a decade ago, it had been decided to establish – more or less as a pilot scheme – married quarters for Africans in the newly developing Free State gold fields. The mine-owners hoped that, if the venture proved successful, they would be allowed gradually to extend it and bring a permanent African mining labour force into existence. This promising development was, however, suppressed by the government, and the mines were eventually allowed to provide married quarters for their essential personnel only up to a maximum of 3 per cent of the total labour employed. In the words of Mr Doxey, who has described this abortive experiment, 'the mining companies were thus compelled to refrain from any attempt, however modest in scope, to build up a settled labour force'.[1]

THE INFLUX OF FOREIGN AFRICAN LABOUR

The problems of migratory labour are complicated by the large proportion of foreign Africans entering from Portuguese East Africa, the Protectorates, Nyasaland and other formerly British colonies as far north as Kenya and Tanganyika. This influx has been increasing steadily in recent years: they are now thought to form two-thirds of the total African labour force in the mines, compared with little over half in 1957.

These Africans have no wish to become immigrants – subjects of the Republic. They regard themselves as 'temporary sojourners'.[2] But had it not been for official

---

son Commission (1951) estimated that the migratory Africans are actually earning (i.e., actually doing paid work) during a period of only about 38 per cent of their working lives.

[1] Doxey, *op. cit.*, pp. 177–8.

[2] This fact gives considerable weight to the argument of the government that the migrant Africans of the Republic must equally be regarded as 'temporary sojourners' in the mining and urban areas.

restraints, the influx of African women from outside South Africa, as well as from the reserves, may well have tended to follow the influx of African men from both sources, in which case large numbers might have become immigrants. Although the result would have increased the magnitude of some problems confronting the town authorities, it would have solved others. *Laissez faire*, by permitting the growth of a normal family life in the areas offering employment, would have increased the attractiveness of mining and industrial work for both indigenous and foreign Africans. Left to themselves, black labourers from all parts of the continent would have trekked towards the opportunities and prospects offered in South Africa, just as the poorer people of Europe sailed across the Atlantic to the United States before the First World War.

Migratory African labour is not rendered cheaper (as is sometimes supposed) because Africans possess a prime source of subsistence in the reserves or in their homelands. Indeed, this factor has exactly the opposite influence by increasing the wage offer necessary to draw and hold the very conservative tribal dwellers away from the environment and social order in which they grew up and would mostly still prefer. For the employers the system is wasteful from almost every angle; and wastefulness spells dearness, not cheapness. Industrialists want a healthy, contented, loyal labour force.

Even in most 'put and carry' work some measure of experience, training and knowledge of routines are important for efficiency. Yet, although migrant Africans usually prefer to return to the same mine or (less frequently) to the same urban employer, their irregularity often obliges them to accept employment wherever there is a satisfactory vacancy, a circumstance which is aggravated by 'influx control'.[1] Productivity must suffer under any such system. Had the Africans been allowed – let alone encouraged – to develop as a normal town community, there can be little doubt that their contribution to the value of work performed would have been incomparably larger. The number of days worked would have increased and output per head have been improved.

---

[1] Official control on the entry of Africans into urban areas. See Chapter 15, pp. 130–1.

LIMITED TRAINING OPPORTUNITIES

Hence, although the free market system has assisted the productive use of unskilled African labour, it has been allowed a very limited success in circumventing legislation, official action, or collusive action tolerated by the state, which has denied opportunities for the Africans to use skill and so effectively destroyed their incentive to acquire skill. This has been wholly to the detriment of industry. For instance, one important form of economy frustrated by regulations under the Mines and Works Act, by closed shop agreements under the Industrial Conciliation Act, and since 1956 by the 'job reservation' clauses of that Act, has been that attainable through 'work studies', under which 'skilled jobs' are analysed and broken down into 'skilled' or 'semi-skilled' operations on the one hand, and truly skilled operations on the other. In South Africa such analysis would normally have led to Africans being allowed to undertake (at first) the 'semi-skilled' parts of the work, thereby releasing Whites and Coloureds for employments demanding relatively more skill. This process, which has been fruitfully utilised in some measure on the Rhodesian copper belt,[1] has been virtually suppressed in the Republic of South Africa. Experience in Northern Rhodesia provides some indication of South Africa's loss in industrial and mining pursuits, and the near future may teach even more salutary lessons about the ability of Africans to contribute to output.[2]

The *apartheid* policy has been increasingly represented as implying separate development, including the provision of facilities for African advancement (economic and political) in 'their own areas'. But when this policy was introduced Africans, who were denied the effective right to be apprenticed,[3] could not – even in the townships and locations where

---

[1] I am not suggesting, of course, that Africans employed in the Rhodesian copper belt have been permitted – by the powerful white labour union – to acquire and exercise skills freely; although a trend in that direction now seems imminent.
[2] Provided, of course, that the necessary disciplinary structure and the market determination of wage-rates are not frustrated.
[3] There is no law to forbid the apprenticeship of Africans who have managed to acquire the necessary educational qualification. But any attempt to do so would almost certainly be quashed by the Registrar of Apprenticeship, responding to labour union pressure.

they were living – legally perform any of a wide range of skilled tasks, in building and other industries, for which many had, often rather surreptitiously, acquired skills.

In 1951, when the conditions under which many Africans were living outside the reserves and mine compounds had led to irritating external criticism, the Native Building Workers' Act was passed to help rectify this disability by providing training facilities in building crafts for Africans. In an industry in which, as labourers, they make up four-fifths of the total labouring force, qualified Africans may now legally act as brick-layers, painters, etc., in 'their own areas' and on farms.[1] They are, however, prohibited from doing this skilled building work in most other urban areas and the government retain complete discretion to determine the maximum number of Africans who may be allowed to acquire building skills.[2]

Even as unskilled labourers, Africans absorbed into the urban economy have obtained considerable benefits, not least in economic security. The tribal life is precarious in the extreme because crop failure (due to drought or pests) or cattle epidemics may cause famine. But because they have no effective labour unions, Africans can easily obtain employment (in urban as well as mine or farm occupations) when they face adversity in their homelands, so long as legislative obstacles do not prevent it. Hence the urban source of income tends to be highly elastic, and acts as a remarkably effective stabiliser in the economy of the reserves.[3]

With the typical Africans, however, it remains difficult to distinguish involuntary unemployment from the consumption of leisure. And sometimes what appears to be unemployment is, properly viewed, employment in the entre-

---

[1] It need hardly be stressed that the farming vote is more powerful than the industrial vote.
[2] By 1961, 3,153 Africans had been authorised to do building work (under these restrictions) and there were 566 official learners.
[3] The present policy of gradually transferring Africans from the urban areas in which their earnings are highest (such as the Western Cape) to badly located 'border areas' (in which their earnings are planned to be much lower – see Chapter 16, pp. 142–3), or to the 'Bantustans', or to farm and mining pursuits, is likely to weaken this source of economic security.

preneurial effort of prospecting for the best paid opportunities. Thus the African may not always accept the first available employment. He may, for instance, prefer to scrape a meagre subsistence in the reserves; or he may prefer to invest in the search for better remunerated openings. If dismissed he seldom needed (until a few years ago) to spend more than a week or so in finding another job in any developed industrial area. Because he was usually confident of finding appropriate employment before long, he would sometimes spend much longer periods in seeking the best opening. In the past he was not forced to accept any job offered; and firms which required additional labour usually knew that they could attract it from other employers by offering generous wage-rates and good conditions of work.

In recent years, however, the position has changed fundamentally. Africans 'endorsed out' of an industrial area and anxious to avoid farming or mining may now find it impossible to discover another region where industrial employment is permitted for them. Unemployment in this sense may conceivably become increasingly serious. Moreover, it is no longer easy for the African to invest time in the search for favourable remuneration and fringe benefits. If he leaves a job he is liable to be 'endorsed out', and if he does get permission to enter an industrial area to look for work, he is allowed only 72 hours in which to do so. Such defects are obviously the product of labour direction, explicitly aimed to obstruct the relatively benevolent operation of the free market.

The Africans who have entered urban employment have had one big advantage compared with other races. Whilst they were excluded, originally by a custom and later by legislation, from preparation for the better-paid opportunities, they were not themselves permitted to organise in labour unions wielding the power of the strike threat.[1] The result was that up to 1946 they came to enjoy, in the sort of industrial work left to them, a steadily increasing proportion of the growing aggregate value of the product of industry, and until 1946, real earnings per head which were increasing more rapidly than those of any other section of the population.

---
[1] They had, of course, no poorer, subservient classes to exploit.

The higher wage-rates offered to Africans in secondary industry are possibly due to the absence of 'monopoly' elements among employers, such as the common recruiting organisation for mining employments. In spite of the absence of labour union organisation for Africans in most of the industries employing them, their labour has throughout been scarce, and managements have found it profitable to outbid one another for the limited supply.[1] This scarcity is even more marked in the industrial regions of the Western Cape because of the distance from the African reserves, and wage-rates would have risen even more above those of other regions were it not that this area appears to have acquired a good reputation among Africans for treating them justly and humanely.

On the other hand, the absence of a common recruiting organisation or of an effective bonus system as a reward for long service seems to have meant that the turnover of African labour in industry and trade has throughout tended to be higher than in the mines. The African seldom feels any loyalty or sense of belonging to the firm which employs him. And although the colour bar has been less blatant and less rigid in industry, permitting exceptionally gifted or enterprising Africans to obtain some measure of responsibility or semi-skilled status, the overwhelming majority have been confined to completely unskilled work requiring mainly muscular strength. Here their labour has been very satisfactory, and apart from the tendency to leave for another job or return to the reserves, they are said to be conscientious, courteous and good-natured employees. Nor

---

[1] Of recent years I am not sure that this assertion has been quite true in the Western Province. The relative scarcity of African labour seems to have led managements to informal agreements not to 'poach' one another's unskilled labour. Over the last decade, African wage-rates in secondary industry and commerce may therefore have been well below their equilibrium value, in the sense that it would have otherwise been profitable to employ far more than were available at the ruling wage-rates. Such a situation was possible because Africans have no effective labour organisation, whereas the wage-rates of white labourers and artisans are mostly covered by Wage Act or by the Industrial Conciliation Act which do not fix the price of African labour. At the same time, during the last few years, influx control (according to the most recent statistics) seems to be having the effect of increasing the *per capita* urban remuneration of Africans still more rapidly than that of other sections.

do they seem resentful of industrial discipline, although it is almost entirely enforced by Whites.[1]

AFRICAN ENTREPRENEURS

One field of African advancement that legislation did not originally discourage was business enterprise. Since the last war, a few thrifty and energetic Africans, perceiving opportunities for profit, have opened shops, dry cleaning establishments, filling stations, garages, cinemas, and simple businesses of that nature. The government has not failed to recognise this tendency to capitalistic development, and has (in 1963) begun to use its arbitrary powers to suppress it. Directives from the Secretary for Bantu Administration and Development have forbidden the opening of any new African owned or directed businesses even in African urban areas. Existing African businesses are to be allowed to continue temporarily, but it is the intention to 'persuade' or 'encourage' their owners to transfer them to the reserves (the Africans' 'homelands'), that is, far away from the areas where most African income is earned and spent. The explanation given is naturally the paternal concern of the government for the welfare of the Africans themselves! Their enterprises are, it is said, 'frequently not successful' and the black public does not, for instance, 'obtain a proper cinema service'. But the real object has clearly been that of preventing the inauguration of African enterprise with its powerful educative influence and its stabilising tendency among the urban Africans.

A final consideration concerns the distinction between the increasing real earnings of Africans and the number enjoying them. Even under the migrant labour system, with standard wage-rates and other colour bars, industrial employment could have raised the average standards of the Africans much more rapidly if their growing aggregate real income had not induced a massive increase in their total population. Is it necessary to insist that one ought not to blame the free market for this? A free labour market can disclose the most productive and best-remunerated oppor-

---

[1] The possibility that Africans usually prefer white foremen is suggested in an unpublished study of Dr van der Horst on the employment of Africans in the Cape Town area.

tunities for the additional hands, to feed, clothe, shelter and amuse the additional bodies. But, *ceteris paribus*, the remuneration will have to be lower the more rapidly the labour force increases.

The inescapable conclusion of this Chapter is that private enterprise in mining and industry (and the same is true even of the less rationally conducted sphere of farming activity) has tended to work wholly for the material advancement (and indirectly the social benefit) of the African people. The intervention of the centralised state, on the other hand, has worked almost entirely in the opposite direction, and the sole exceptions are found in certain mitigations of restraints on African labour and in the provision of urban amenities – policies introduced to ease consciences, to satisfy world opinion or to stave off internal trouble.[1]

This reality is strikingly illustrated by the case of migrant or foreign Africans who are prepared to travel huge distances in order to take advantage of the opportunities of earning which are offered in the Republic. The remarkable current influx of foreign African labour to the mines, in spite of the Republic's appalling reputation, is significant. There are now over 800,000 black aliens in the Republic, all of whom are perfectly free to leave, or not to return after periodical sojourns at home, if their own independent countries can offer them better opportunities. But never before have they seemed to be as anxious as they are today to take advantage of the demand for their labour in the land which all African states unite in damning. Notwithstanding vociferous official hostility to the Republic's policies, the countries from which the foreign Africans are attracted have been unable to prevent their nationals, impoverished through decolonisation, from flocking in ever-increasing numbers to mining and other employments. Even the recently enforced closing of the mines' recruitment organisation in Tanganyika has so far failed to stem the influx of Tanganyikans into the Republic; and the prospect of the South African Government, for political reasons, forbidding the entry of Basutos has created alarm in Basutoland because

---

[1] For example, in the Native Building Workers' Act, and in some aspects of Bantustan policy.

any such action would threaten that Protectorate with starvation.[1]

Under the Aliens Control Act of 1963, the Government of the Republic has acquired increased powers of exclusion, on the grounds of doing justice to its own Africans.[2] In a debate on the measure a Nationalist speaker referred to its being used to create employment at home by withdrawing opportunities for aliens. No wonder that a wise Basuto from Maseru is reported to have said:

'They talk of independence! When freedom comes, my job may be placed in jeopardy and I could be out of work ... By stopping this flow of labour South Africa could cripple the country in a month without touching other things like transport and communications.'[3]

---

[1] About half the alien Africans in the Republic come from the Protectorates, and over 150,000 of them are Basutos. The latter are an important source of labour for the Johannesburg mines, where they have acquired considerable competence and experience as shaft-sinkers.

[2] A passport will be needed in future.

[3] *Cape Argus*, 7 May, 1963. The Government of the Republic could also withhold the 0.88 per cent of her customs revenues which, by an agreement concluded at Union, is at present paid to the Protectorates. This makes up one-third of Basutoland's revenues, one-fifth of Bechuanaland's and one-tenth of Swaziland's.

CHAPTER 11

AFRICANS AND LABOUR UNIONS

EVEN without the intervention of law, effective combination among African labourers would have been difficult because of high labour turnover due to the migratory system, marked language and tribal differences, the paternalistic governmental system of their reserve homelands, their general naïvety and the absence of any *tradition* resembling labour-union action. In the early years of this century, when really powerful workers' combinations had been established in the mines by the Whites, the Africans remained without any apparent form of organisation as a pressure group. In 1911, this state of affairs was perpetuated by legislation which rendered legal strike action almost impossible.

How has this disability adversely affected the relative or absolute standards of the Africans? This question can be answered only in the light of a recognition that consumers are the ultimate employers, and that strike power can, in the long run, increase the remuneration of any group of workers only through (i) the exclusion of some of its competitors, or (ii) through forcing the removal of exclusive barriers imposed against the group by its competitors (or by the state on its competitors' behalf) but not through the exclusion of the complementary resources supplied by investors.[1]

To those who perceive the implications of this vital principle, it must appear that the biggest blunder made by the people who were trying to maintain the Africans in their traditional subservience was in not permitting them to organise in labour unions with the right to strike. It could easily have been pleaded that the simple Africans entering the modern world needed protection against exploitation; and moralists the world over would have

---
[1] See pp. 107–8.

eulogised this enlightened attitude. Yet the result of effective African labour unions would have been the attainment by a relatively small group of black employees of far higher standards of living, whilst the vast majority of Africans (a smaller number because the population survival would have been much reduced) would have remained in the relatively poverty-striken reserves or on the farms.

Such a policy would have perpetuated both rural and urban poverty among the Whites as well as further impoverishing non-Whites. The industrial progress which, as we have seen, has come about through the rapid economic integration of all races since the 1930s, would have been drastically slowed down; the unprecedented farming prosperity enjoyed until recently (in spite of enhanced farm wage-rates) through the more effective use of the non-white people in industry would have been sacrificed. But many South Africans would not regard poverty and backwardness among the Whites (if accompanied by a parallel decline in non-white standards) as too big a price to pay for the certainty of the perpetual subordination of Africans.

AVOIDANCE OF UNION RESTRICTIONS

The first law which made it virtually illegal to organise strikes among Africans was the Native Labour Regulation Act of 1911. This Act, which resembles in some ways the Masters' and Servants' Acts (see below, p. 106), includes also some admirable provisions regulating recruitment organisations, defining the liability of the mines in respect of injuries (along the lines of workmen's compensation) and prescribing minimum standards in respect of other fringe compensations (health conditions, medical facilities, compound accommodation and food) for Africans. The Act applies to any area or industry the government may determine.

Strikes and lock-outs by Africans were not expressly forbidden by law until 1953, although the Native Labour (Settlement of Disputes) Act of that year did little more than provide iron-clad consolidation of a situation which had prevented African labour unions from functioning aggressively since the beginning of the century. The hope was openly expressed that, by providing other machinery for handling industrial relations, the Act would finally undermine African labour unions[1] (which, although 'unrecognised', had always been legal organisations unless they resorted to strikes or strike threats). The new machinery consists principally of Regional Labour Committees, under white chairmen, to which selected Africans are appointed by the Minister of Labour – not elected. These Regional Committees, which are intended to mediate in the case of disputes, fall under the Central Native Labour Board. It is provided also that African employees in a factory shall have the right to elect works committees to express their wishes.

The laws against strike action have been extraordinarily effective. In spite of political organisations like the African National Congress and the Pan African Congress (which became so powerful that they were recently declared illegal), there appear to have been no successful and few attempted strikes on the part of African employees.[2] Such minor strikes as have occurred have probably been due, almost entirely, to indignation at grievances which were quite unconnected with remuneration or fringe benefits. But where African labour unions have been established, managements seem to have taken their existence into account and to have been anxious to be on good terms with them. Such unions have, on occasion, presented the Africans' viewpoint before the Wage Board, under the Wage Act.

Now these laws and circumstances which, through denying Africans the right to protect groups among themselves from the competition of their many compatriots, have so assisted African advancement as a whole, may yet be held to have been 'unfair'. This is because they have, at the same time, withheld also the power to fight similar exclusions imposed by other labour unions, by industrial councils or through the Wage Act. Hence, although Africans have no legitimate grievance at having been denied permission to raise labour costs in the occupations in which they work, they do have, it seems to me, a very genuine grievance in that the law has permitted organisation on the part of other races to raise their labour costs; for the labour organisations

---

[1] This has not happened.
[2] In 1959, 221 Africans were convicted under the 1953 Act.

of Whites and Coloureds, together with direct protections and demarcations imposed by the state, have not only raised the prices of the commodities which the Africans have to buy but have reduced the latters' opportunities of bidding for more productive and well-remunerated work.

At the same time the Africans as a whole have been protected against exploitation by labour unions organised by those of their own race; and this protection has always threatened to bring about effective ultimate competition of Africans with Whites and Coloureds. The threat has been intensified by fears of the eventual results of Bantustans and developments in the Rhodesias and has recently caused apprehension in white labour unions, which have begun to suggest that African unions should now be 'recognised' under the Industrial Conciliation Act. To prevent African advancement through effective competition with the Whites (they say, of course, to 'prevent the exploitation of Africans to the detriment of white organised labour') the white unions want Africans to have active unions of their own.[1] There is a real danger that this request will soon be acceded to, for it would perpetuate the economic subordinancy of the black races in a way the world will approve. The authorities are likely to fear also that, if effective labour unions are prohibited, the Africans will join politically motivated – perhaps underground – associations. The African leaders are unlikely to perceive the purpose in any such move. Today's ideologies and stereotypes have prevented them, as well as their white advisers (with a few interesting but unimportant exceptions), from perceiving that the free market would have offered the opportunities which restraints on the market have denied to them. The law, the administration and the tolerance of collusive labour action have held off these opportunities.

The Africans have throughout had some rights under the Masters' and Servants' Acts which are likely to be repealed under the Bantu Laws Amendment Bill. They seem to have become anachronistic, not because the time has been thought ripe for the concession of the right of collective bargaining to Africans, but because other means of pre-

---
[1]This point of view was clearly expressed at the ninth General Meeting of the Trade Union Council of South Africa, held in May, 1963.

venting discontent among African employees, superficially similar to those believed to be normal behind the Iron Curtain, are about to be adopted.

When their work has competed (currently or potentially) with that of other races, the remuneration of Africans has been determined through Industrial Council Agreements (to which, of course, the Africans themselves are not parties) or under the Wage Act. In some Wage Board determinations the bulk of all of the employees covered by the determination have been Africans. This machinery has almost certainly had the effect of curbing not only the entry of Africans into industrial and commercial employments (from farming and mining), but still more their rates of progress into semi-skilled or skilled work.

Amendments made to the Industrial Conciliation Act in 1956 may, however, conceivably have the wholly unintended effect of encouraging organisations which might enable non-Whites to exercise countervailing coercive power against economic colour bars. These amendments enact that Whites and non-Whites may not be members of the same labour unions,[1] except in separate branches of mixed unions which must have wholly white executives.[2] And with separate non-white unions, it could happen that the power of the strike was used to achieve the right to perform work at present monopolised by Whites. That is, the non-white unions might prove capable of breaking the oppressive power of the standard rate principle by achieving the right to undercut. If so, they could dissolve the economic injustices which the enforcement of so-called 'equal pay for equal work' has perpetrated and perpetuated. Indeed, reports of friction between the racially split unions suggest that attempts in this direction are already being made. On the other hand, the amended Industrial Conciliation Act of 1956 (to say nothing of the Bantu Laws Amendment Bill) confers ministerial powers like those

---

[1] In the case of very small labour unions, the Minister of Labour may use his extraordinarily sweeping powers to grant exemption from this requirement.

[2] Members of different races in mixed unions are not permitted to be present at meetings at which Whites are present. The sole exception is executive meetings, where non-Whites may legally be present in order to state their point of view.

which, we are told, are wielded by the state in the Iron Curtain countries; and this may rule out the possibility to which I have here referred.

THE MASTERS' AND SERVANTS' ACTS

The absence of labour unions has not meant that Africans have had no protection against abuse by managements of firms or individual employers. In the Afrikaner Republics, as well as in the Cape and Natal, the Masters' and Servants' Acts had previously aimed to protect the labouring classes (mainly Africans but to some extent Coloureds and Indians) from possible abuses by their employers, because they (the non-Whites) could not effectively enforce contracts through civil actions, and *vice versa*. On the face of it, one would have thought that the labourers had more to gain than their employers from simple machinery for the enforcement of employment agreements when privately initiated proceedings against either parties would have been impracticable. In principle, protection was provided for the employee as much as for the employer. In practice, it is believed by many to have operated most unfairly for the non-Whites.

It may be mainly because the non-Whites have provided the bulk of the labouring force that the idea has arisen of these laws constituting a clear case of colour injustice. The use of criminal sanctions (against 'masters' as well as against 'servants') for the enforcement of contract is certainly reminiscent of communist institutions. But the intention of the Masters' and Servants' laws was good: they embodied the wisdom of experience, evolved from attempts to solve genuine problems, and in content do not suggest discrimination. Any real injustices must have arisen more out of the administration of the law. For instance, it has been alleged that, particularly in the villages, the popularity of the magistrates who enforce these laws has often depended upon the severity with which they deal with the employees.

If laws of this kind are wisely conceived and justly administered, there is a legitimate role for labour unions. They can provide machinery for the effective enforcement of the legal rights of their members so as to ensure that contracts of employment are entered into freely, and subsequently honoured.

On the whole, however, criticism of the Masters' and Servants' Acts seems to have sprung from the popular notion that the private exercise of coercive power (*via* strike or other action)[1] constitutes one of the basic rights of man in a free society. These laws are often regarded as 'antiquated' largely because, if they can in fact provide effective court protection against abuses, they have dissolved the fashionable arguments in favour of the toleration of private coercion. But disputes about the fulfilment of contracts between the employee and the people as consumers (concerning the wages and other compensation he is entitled to expect from consumers) ought surely to be settled without recourse to industrial war or the threat to use it. Is it not better to allow independent courts to interpret agreements *and to ensure that they have been freely entered into?* Is it not better to allow the determination of wage-rates and the conditions of work without recourse to the principle of 'might is right'? Admittedly, safeguards are desirable against the exploitation of one set of employees by others, such as by the managers against the rank and file. But ought not these safeguards to be embodied into non-discriminatory rules the breach of which can be challenged by appeal to the courts?

A common argument for the retention of the Masters' and Servants' Acts and other Acts embodying the same principle (like the Native Labour Regulation Act of 1911) is that the classes to whom this legislation applies have not yet reached the standard of civilisation and responsibility which would justify their being entrusted with coercive power (the right to collective bargaining). This argument implies that they must, sooner or later, progress to the stage at which it will be thought appropriate to grant permission for Africans to arm for private economic war (for righteous aggression or defence). But I am by no means certain that, if they had possessed such powers, the Africans would have used them less irresponsibly or less anti-socially than the Whites have used them in the Western world in general. For one thing, the Communists would certainly have man-

---

[1] As we have seen, such action compels consumers to pay more for output, or suppresses competition from (i.e., opportunities for) less fortunate classes.

œuvred to get control of African labour unions and they would, I think, have succeeded. We can guess that they would have done their best to foster the quite understandable bitterness of the Africans; any such outcome would have been just as indefensible as the 'Colour Bar Acts' which political agitators had successfully demanded through the strikes of 1907 and 1922, and the civilised labour – *apartheid* trend established under the Labour-Nationalist pact of 1924.

Naturally, it appears to be grossly unfair to deny any labouring class and especially the Africans the right to organise when these rights are permitted for other classes and races. And yet virtually the only legislative provisions which have facilitated the rise of the Africans in the economic sphere have been those which have prohibited or otherwise hindered their right to strike. It seems to me that all other industrial legislation in South Africa (with the sole exception of the Masters' and Servants' Acts) has tended in the opposite direction, namely, to maintain the non-Whites in a condition of economic inferiority and subordinancy. It is natural enough that the Africans and their leaders should deeply resent their inability to use the power of the strike whilst others have that right. But, as we have seen, unless they could use strike power (a) to force the state to abandon those restraints on the free market which have borne so unfairly upon them; or (b) to break such economic power as is possessed by the white labour unions, they could as a group gain nothing thereby. On the other hand, if they attempted to better their condition by fighting the 'profit-seeking capitalist' they would merely prolong their economic subjection.

The use of labour union power to crush labour union power does, however, seem to be a distinct possibility in the not too distant future in a neighbouring country because the white and black unions there are separate organisations. The African Mineworkers Union in Northern Rhodesia (with 35,000 members) has recently demanded the 'Africanisation' of mining operations, including the right to training for responsible and skilled work such as surveyors and draughtsmen. The fact that the mining management agreed, and accepted African trainees, led to a strike on the part of the 600 white miners at Mufulira,[1] although both management and strikers kept up the pretence that this was not actually the issue.[2] What is interesting is that the management held out against the Whites for more than two months and eventually won the struggle on behalf of the Africans. They did not want the strike to continue, of course, but they obviously recognised that, in the era which was emerging, any strike against colour bars which had been imposed by white union pressure would have the sympathy of the black-dominated government; and that the Africans must therefore be gradually allowed to undertake skilled and responsible work. Indeed, the owners are almost certainly contemplating the time, in the not too far distant future, when a carefully selected minority of well-educated Africans will have to be trained for top management.

---

[1] This is the world's second largest underground copper mine.
[2] The pretence was that the strike was concerned with the refusal of the white miners to provide data for the payment of bonuses to Africans and other data required for costing.

CHAPTER 12

THE GROUP AREAS POLICY

THE *apartheid* (in English 'separateness') policy under that name was introduced by the Nationalist Party after their victory in the 1948 elections. There was nothing essentially new about it at first, but in its subsequent enactment it has undergone some remarkable changes of emphasis. As an election slogan, it had succeeded because it placed chief stress on white 'baasskap' (i.e., 'mastership'). But partly because of the wish to meet external criticism, from the United Nations and elsewhere, and partly owing to intractable internal developments, increasing emphasis has since been laid upon the notion of 'separate development'. Moreover, there has been a significant change of tone in government utterances. Some leading advocates of *apartheid* have even been publicly preaching the desirability of courtesy in dealing with Africans, an attitude almost unimaginable 15 years ago. These changes represent retreats in a policy which, it was originally believed, could assist the maintenance of permanent White supremacy, partly by making the non-Whites themselves recognise their inherent inferiority.

LEGISLATING FOR APARTHEID
Among the measures which sought to entrench *apartheid* by such means is the Group Areas Act of 1950. The chief aim of this Act, which has created the most extreme bitterness, in spite of a whole series of amendments (some mitigating, some aggravating) is to establish and enforce segregation in respect of residence, property and business ownership.[1] This is not a wholly preposterous objective. To some extent,

---

[1] The group which has been most adversely affected economically by the Group Areas legislation has been the Indians, for they have very largely built up their businesses and goodwill in white areas. I devote Chapter 14 to their special case.

racial segregation occurs purely as a result of natural human preference. It is very common in the world to find urban districts in which Chinese, Japanese, Indians, Syrians, Jews or other groups have congregated because of the preference of the poorer races for residence in the cheaper areas, the desire to avoid the unpleasantness of race prejudice or the wish to live near or as part of their own racially defined community. These tendencies had been traditionally enforced in South Africa by private covenants under which the sale of land or property to non-Whites was excluded by contract. The Group Areas Act has mainly affected the districts in which such contractually enforced segregation has not occurred. It not only restricts, on a racial basis, the areas of future development but sets out to enforce segregation in formerly mixed areas.

When the Coloured people and Indians have been forced to move from one district to another under the Act, they have normally been given adequate notice;[1] and accommodation in new areas, often superior and not more expensive, has been available. But it has nearly always left them further from their place of employment;[2] and the motive has made compulsory transfer an affront. Moreover, the Group Areas mentality ignores 'the feeling of belonging, and the security of moving around in a well-known territory', considerations which 'are important to men, as they are to birds and animals'.[3]

The Minister of Coloured Affairs has recently claimed that the Government's real aim is the 'eventual removal of racial discrimination by allowing the various groups to develop and progress in their own areas'. But they certainly do not yet contemplate, for instance, the gradual admission of Coloureds to equality of opportunity in respect of the

---

[1] Removal notices are not usually served until at least one year after Group Area proclamations, and the notices must then give a minimum of three months' grace in respect of residences and twelve months in respect of businesses.

[2] This movement of non-Whites to areas further and further from their place of employment has been most serious in the case of Africans. It seems to have had some effect upon industrial location, some new factories having been sited so as to be near to where the African employees live.

[3] Wilson and Mafaje, *op. cit.*, p. 173.

better-paid employments in 'their own areas'. Indeed, because most Group Areas enactments have forced the Coloureds to live further than formerly from their work, they are likely to mean the withholding of opportunity.

One of the latest proclamations under the Act threatens the disruption of the lives of 5,000 Indians and the ruin of nearly 200 Indian businesses. They are to be expelled from an area in Johannesburg which has been one of their principal trading districts for more than half a century – indeed, since the days of Kruger. This area had been explicitly set aside for non-White occupation, with rights conferred in 1902 and 1941 to acquire freehold property. It contains two mosques, five Indian religious schools and various Indian amenities. Will it be surprising if this move leaves a smouldering indignation? The only group area for Indians in the Johannesburg district is to be at Lenasia, 22 miles outside the city.

BITTER LEGACY OF SEGREGATION
The resentments aroused by such imposed territorial segregation are due only partly to any economic injustice so caused. Well-to-do and well-educated Coloured people, Indians and Africans, are mostly convinced that the aim has been deliberately to humiliate them, to express contempt by a measure intended to emphasise, to them and to society, their inferiority and subordinacy. Thus, the various non-white races have almost invariably been moved or confined to the less pleasant districts. Explicit amendments of the original Act have laid it down that the facilities provided for non-Whites need not be 'separate but equal'– merely 'separate'. In coastal towns, the beaches made available to the non-Whites have been the unattractive and least accessible ones; indeed, they have been banned from beaches and public parks they previously enjoyed whenever the Whites have coveted them. On publicly-owned transport they have been segregated into separate compartments, separate entrances, separate ticket offices, separate cloakrooms, etc. In the Cape Province where, before the enforcement of the Group Areas legislation, there had been no colour bar on the state-owned railways, on the local services, segregation was clearly intended to demonstrate that

the non-Whites were regarded more or less as social lepers likely to contaminate the Whites if they travelled in the same buses, or on adjacent seats in buses, or in the same railway compartments. A further discriminatory rule implying disparagement concerns the right to use African domestic servants: the employment of Africans in this capacity is permitted in white areas only. And in the same spirit, the Factories Act was amended in 1960 to confer even more sweeping powers on the Minister of Labour to enforce the physical separation of the different race groups employed in any undertaking.

This emphasis on inferiority of status which is so resented by the non-Whites is illustrated by a general principle in all the Nationalist Government's race legislation, namely, that no White shall ever be expected to hold any post where he will be subordinate to a non-White. Thus, in some 'group areas', firms owned by non-Whites may not employ Whites.[1] And it is in keeping with this approach that the Minister of Bantu Administration recently issued a directive that 'no official shall shake hands with a black man'. Similarly, the Defence Act provides that no non-Whites (i.e., the Coloureds, the Indians or Africans) shall ever be deemed to be the superior officer of any White, so that no non-White of any rank will ever be in a position to give orders to a White. And in the state-subsidised hospitals no non-white doctor may give instructions to white nurses.

The humiliation of non-Whites through the Group Areas legislation has been further emphasised in (a) the Immorality Act, which makes sexual intercourse or intimacy between Whites and non-Whites (even if the couple have married since the Act was passed) a criminal offence,[2] although relations between, say, Coloureds and Africans, or between Indians and Africans, constitute no crime; (b) the Prohibition of Mixed Marriages Act, which forbids intermarriage between Whites and non-Whites yet permits inter-

---

[1] In view of the fact that, as yet, there is a relative handful of experienced non-white executives in South Africa, this rule must make it extraordinarily difficult to establish businesses under non-white ownership or management.

[2] Indeed, an even more serious offence than homosexual relations in most countries.

marriage between the other non-white races; (c) the exclusion of non-white students from those universities which had formerly accepted them,[1] separate university colleges under stringent state control being provided for the non-white races; (d) governmental pressure to enforce *apartheid* even in scientific and learned societies;[2] (e) the enforced segregation of non-Whites and Whites in the Cape Town city libraries which, until 1963, were open to all races;[3] (f) the Population Register Act, in terms of which the registration cards which all are supposed to carry specify one's race.

It must be admitted, however, that *apartheid* of the group areas kind has to some extent created (hardly intentionally) opportunities for non-Whites to serve their own people in government employment, in grades which were formerly virtually denied to them, although at lower remuneration than is paid to Whites. They have been allowed, for instance, in clerical and minor executive posts on the railways, where they have to deal only with their own racial group. Again, in the separate university colleges for non-Whites, the more able Coloureds, Indians and Africans may well find opportunities (at lower salaries) which the 'open universities', selecting staff according to academic achievement and promise alone, would never have been able to offer them;[4] and because these universities are cheaper, higher education (inferior and – some of us fear – indoc-

---

[1] The universities concerned bitterly opposed this legislation. They remain 'open universities' and have pledged themselves to continue to press for the restoration of their right to admit or reject students on the basis of academic merit, not colour or race.

[2] The Minister of Education, Arts and Science has recently informed these societies that, unless they discharge from membership any non-Whites among them, they will lose all state subsidies. Most learned societies will, it is believed, forgo their subsidies rather than take this step, which some have suggested will not only bring South Africa into ridicule abroad, but cause valuable scientific and cultural links with the world to be lost. Non-white membership has not, however, yet been made illegal.

[3] The threat to withdraw the Provincial subsidy was the method of enforcement.

[4] The staffs of the university colleges for non-Whites are, at present, almost entirely White.

trinated)[1] may be brought more effectively within the reach of the poorer races. And it is certainly not out of the question that *apartheid* in other forms will indirectly have similar consequences and provide, so to speak, politically acceptable ways of reducing colour injustice, especially in the 'border industries' and 'Bantustan' developments (see Chapters 16 and 17). But the spheres in which this will be possible appear to be few and limited by political expediency in a régime in which the votes of Coloureds are unimportant and those of Indians and Africans non-existent.[2]

THE TYRANNY OF PARLIAMENTARY MAJORITIES

It may be thought that residential segregation and separate facilities in respect of universities, libraries, learned societies, beaches, public gardens, the Post Office, theatres, sport, transport, etc., are hardly examples of injustices of *economic* origin; for in these cases any discriminatory treatment appears to originate in political or socio-psychological factors rather than economic causes. But it is an important part of my case that all forms of what are felt to be injustices – economic or otherwise – can be seen to have their ultimate source in an abuse of parliamentary majorities. For majorities, even if based on 'one man, one vote', may withdraw from minorities or from classes not represented the opportunity to win equal dignity and respect as well as the right to economic opportunities.

This is, I feel, the most vital point of my whole thesis. Unless parliaments are restrained by iron-clad constitutional entrenchments, political majorities, as defined and distorted by electoral laws and voting procedures, will almost always be tempted to exploit their power tyranically, that is, without true regard for the rights or feelings of political minorities or for those who lack effective political representation. The majorities in the white constituencies,

---

[1] The university colleges for non-Whites are as much under direct governmental control as they are in Communist countries. Professors and lecturers have the status of public servants. It is difficult to know what measure of freedom of thought is possible under these conditions.

[2] It remains true, I think, that as long as it is within the power of the Government to protect Whites from the competition of non-Whites, the right of the latter to contribute to the common pool of output is almost certain to be restrained at least as much as it has been in the past.

to which the authors of the Group Areas programme have successfully appealed, have *wanted* to humiliate the non-Whites. Let us be under no illusion on that point. This is partly because one of the parties found it profitable deliberately to foster racial pride, racial prejudices, racial fears and racial hatreds. But do not the almost sadistic aspects of the laws I have been discussing expose the undemocratic weakness of certain forms of representative governmental machinery? I return to this problem in Chapter 18.

CHAPTER 13

JOB RESERVATION

IN harmony with the spirit of the 'group areas' policy has been the incorporation of overt 'job reservation' into the Industrial Conciliation Act by amendments introduced in 1956 and 1959. This step has rendered more specific and deliberate the exclusions which had previously been stealthily achieved through the standard rate principle since the inception of the Act in 1924 and quite honestly through the Mines and Works Act of 1926 and the Native Building Workers' Act of 1951. It has tended to determine the broad occupational structure of society by authority instead of the market, and on a racial basis instead of by trainable ability. One consequence has been (especially since the 1959 amendment) that any powers which Coloured employees may have come to acquire under the original Industrial Conciliation Act of 1924 have now been rendered of little or no effect. In 1957 it had been possible for a Coloured union to strike (legally, although not successfully) against job reservation. The possibility of similar legal resistance in future has now been removed.

ARBITRARY POWERS OF JOB RESTRICTION

In introducing the 'job reservation' amendments, the Nationalists did not refrain from appealing to the emotions aroused by the term 'exploitation'. Their object, they claimed, was to protect the white man from exploitation by the other races – that is, by the less privileged classes with lower standards. Naturally they persevered with the hypocrisy of being equally concerned with the well-being of all. Under the Act, the Minister of Labour is given power to act in the interests of all employees, irrespective of their race or colour, to defend them from inter-racial competition. How obviously just and fair such arbitrary powers can always be represented to be! But the Minister is in fact authorised to reserve defined types of work for particular races alone; that is, he may forbid that any specified kind of job shall be performed by people of any specified race, or enact that it shall be reserved for a particular race. Within the discriminatory determinations so enacted, even the numbers of the various race groups who may be employed can be dictated by him. One provision actually authorises determinations which may remove the right of any race to a form of employment which it has long enjoyed.[1] And the fact that the majority of the employees in the specific jobs reserved for Whites are at present Whites does not alter the fact that the reservation denies, on ground of colour not of skill, the right of non-Whites to qualify for some of the better-paid openings in an industry.

The latest job reservation as I write has specified seven crafts in the building trade[2] which (at the request of two all-white labour unions) may not in the future be undertaken by Coloured employees in the Western Cape (and certain other districts in the Cape and Natal). Yet the Coloured make up 75 per cent of the building artisans in the Western Cape.

The Minister is advised in respect of job reservation by an Industrial Tribunal established by the Act but, as has become typical of legislation under the cult of state intervention, he and his advisers have been accorded the widest powers, including almost unrestricted rights of discrimination (i) between areas (which means, of course, between constituencies), (ii) between individual undertakings (which will make managements wary of openly opposing governmental policies), and (iii) between different industries (which may force industrial associations to feel that they must be obsequious or subservient to the Minister), etc. The Act goes so far as to declare that the tribunal 'may use

---

[1]The following are among some of the job reservations which have already been made in favour of the Whites in certain areas: lift attendants (elevator operators); drivers of transport vehicles in certain spheres; ambulance drivers (even when carrying non-Whites); traffic policemen (where non-Whites had rendered excellent service for some time previously, in Cape Town); firemen; barmen.

[2]The seven crafts are: stone masonry; marble masonry; joinery; woodworking machinery; electrical wiring; letter cutting and stone decoration; shop, office and bank fittings.

any method of differentiation or discrimination it may deem expedient'.

COLOUR–BLIND MARKET *versus* INTERVENTION

It is in arbitrary frustrations of the profit system, imposed through delegated legislation or administrative jurisdiction of this nature, that some of the most serious forms of colour injustice are being currently maintained. Every discrimination explicity authorised in the detail of 1956 and 1959 amendments of the Act is of a type which clearly aims at preventing entrepreneurs from substituting, for the collective benefit, the least-cost method of achieving any kind of demanded output; and that means, in the sphere covered by the Act, preventing managements (under the discipline of the loss-avoidance, profit-seeking incentives) from making the most productive use of the powers of the people.[1]

It may be objected, of course, that job reservations represent a mere abuse of state authority. But without government intervention to restrain the movement of labour, could such discriminations persist in a market that is colour-blind and race-blind?

The actual development of job reservation determination will occur according to the way in which the present and future governments exercise the virtually totalitarian discretion which Parliament has conferred on them; but under the necessity of winning elections with wholly white constituencies, it seems that the almost inevitable outcome will be the imposition upon industry in general of explicit colour bars similar to those incorporated in the Mines and Works Act of 1926 by the Labour-Nationalist Pact Government. As the *Cape Times* recently commented in discussing job reservation, 'it is always at the bread and butter level where most votes are likely to be gained, that the Coloured

---

[1] One of the main reasons for the discriminatory powers assumed in the Industrial Conciliation Act amendments of 1956 and 1959 appears to have been a wish to ensure that, in times of developing depression, the non-Whites (i.e. the non-voters) shall be deprived of their jobs before any of the Whites. But it will not work as easily as this in practice. Without the cheap labour of Africans and other non-Whites, more employment openings for Whites will be destroyed than will be created. On the other hand, the intention of some job reservations already made seems to have been to 'create employment' for unemployed Whites.

people are most discriminated against'.[1] And in Natal it is the Indians who may now expect to be increasingly prejudiced. The latest determination, which withdraws from them the right to serve as barmen (although they may still serve drinks in hotel lounges), seems to be an indication of what is in prospect.

---

[1] *Cape Times*, 1 May, 1963.

CHAPTER 14

THE INDIANS

THE Indian community, of whom about four-fifths live in Natal and most of the rest in the Transvaal, can be clearly differentiated from the Coloured population through their physical features and sociological traits. They constitute the group which, in the absence of restraints on the free market, could most easily be assimilated into the white-dominated occupations and into white society. As with other sections of the population, a large proportion has been attracted to urban from rural pursuits – especially when economic opportunity has weakened or dissolved race prejudice. In so far as they have been able to circumvent the barriers imposed by law and administration, the Indians appear to have adapted themselves to the town environment more successfully than any other groups who have migrated from the countryside; yet, even so, their living conditions in the towns have often been extremely backward.[1] That has been the penalty of poverty. It is not a racial vice. On the other hand, the South African Indians have enjoyed a tradition of racial pride and a transmitted understanding of the art of trade not dissimilar to that preserved through the ages in the Jewish ghettos. Under unrestrained market activity, the Indians would have seized their opportunities, and the slum aspects of their residential areas would then, I think, have been more rapidly eradicated than among any other similarly placed group.

The more successful of the Indians have prospered through trade, usually in retail stores; but a growing proportion has been attracted into secondary industrial activity in Natal. The less successful have obtained employment as waiters (in which craft they excel), as barmen, as domestic servants, in fishing or in plantations and farming

---

[1]Overcrowding has been aggravated by restraints (similar to those of the Group Areas legislation) imposed *before* the *apartheid* era.

work. Some of the better educated have become doctors, attorneys and advocates.

RESENTMENT OF INDIAN ABILITIES

That the background, habits and education of this group make them more easily assimilable into the white man's traditional occupations than any other non-white group seems temporarily to have aggravated enormously the influence of racial prejudice. In this case, fear of competition is probably the chief cause; and it is every bit as strong a factor among the mainly English-speaking Whites of Natal, as it is among the mainly Afrikaans-speaking Whites of the Transvaal. In a market economy the South African Indians would, there is little doubt, have made excellent business men; and the fact that, even under the existing régime, many have been highly successful has engendered jealousy, indignation and even alarm among their white competitors. It is not surprising that the sort of charges of sharp practice which are almost universally made against small-scale Jewish, Syrian, Chinese, Greek or Italian immigrant traders, when they have formed interloping trading classes, have been made against the Indians of Natal and the Transvaal. But as the abuses alleged are nearly all of a kind which could be prevented by the effective enforcement of existing law, it seems probable that the typical charges are at any rate exaggerated.

In part, those who complain are naïvely protesting at the economies which the small Indian traders have achieved, or reproaching them either for their industry and shrewdness or for their initial poverty. Because their inherited penury has not destroyed their ambition, they have typically expressed a very low demand for leisure (in striking contrast to most urban Africans). The willingness of, say, an Indian shopkeeper and his family to serve the public at all hours has tended to be regarded (by his white competitors) as a vice rather than as a virtue. And his alleged dishonesty – unconfirmed by my own rather limited dealing with Indian shops – is unlikely to prove an enduring quality; for every trading class comes to learn that it is subject to the discipline exerted by continuity of dealings. When there is lasting competition between outlets, any 'prudent dealer' would in Adam Smith's words 'rather choose to lose what he has a right to than give ground for suspicion of sharp practice'.[1]

I am not convinced that the Indian retailers have indulged in more dubious business practices than most other small traders, but I am convinced that their competition has reduced the cost of retail services for all residents of Natal. Through their diligence and efficiency they have often triumphed over colour hatred and envy. Their customers have included well-to-do Whites purchasing in cheap markets as well as the less well-off among both Whites and non-Whites; but it is in the service of the poorest classes, in the villages as well as in the towns, that their contribution to the common welfare has been largest. They have provided, in particular, the types and locations of retailing activity which have been well suited for customers of low and irregular incomes, or in thinly populated districts. But, as so often with those engaged in trade, they have been all too apt to be regarded as exploiters and profiteers;[2] and they are far from popular with the people for whom they have probably rendered the largest benefits, namely, the Africans.

African antagonism was, indeed, so powerful in 1948 that anti-Indian riots occurred. The origins of the deep hostility which the Indians had obviously aroused among the Africans have been much discussed but remain (for me at least) obscure, although the Indians are prone to clannishness. But we find this with every minority group which has felt itself to be culturally isolated in a more or less foreign environment; and the clannishness tends to break down in any community which treats all its citizens with equal consideration. Perhaps the resentment of Africans was aroused because, although sometimes equally black, the Indians could not help making it clear that they regarded themselves as a higher race. The majority are descendants of low caste Indians, but in South Africa they had mostly

---

[1] Adam Smith, *Lectures*, Ed. Cannan, p. 255.
[2] The Indians do not appear to have any organisation which would have permitted effective collusive action, although it has been alleged that they have made agreements which operate to the detriment of white competitors.

achieved material standards and a degree of respect within their own community incomparably superior to those they could have expected in their less progressive homeland. It would be a very natural tendency therefore for them to regard themselves as a superior caste to the relatively primitive Africans, and to adopt an attitude which the latter could easily regard as arrogance. In this respect they may have been no better or wiser than the Whites.

APARTHEID AND THE INDIANS

Such status as the Indians have achieved in the South African community has depended mainly upon the impracticability, until recently, of closing the retail avenues of advancement to them, as legislation and custom had closed other openings. It was the scope left to them in this sphere which enabled many Indians to progress through their entrepreneurial initiative, assiduity and thrift. It has been the state which, originally through the Asiatic Land Tenure Act of 1946 and, since 1948, through the development of the '*apartheid* policy' in general and the 'group areas' legislation in particular, has begun to close many of the trading channels of advancement; and it has been doing so by effective restraints on the free market system. In the cause of racial segregation (under the Group Areas Act) Indian traders are being removed from the most profitable trading sites,[1] whilst the issue of additional trading licences to Indians has virtually ceased. It is too early to know whether or to what extent this has meant, or will mean, commercial ruin.[2] But the Prime Minister recently warned Indians that they would gradually have to move away from commerce into other avenues of employment.

The usual phrases are used to justify all these steps. The world is told that there are plans for permitting the Indians to develop 'along their own social, economic and political lines'. But this means only that autonomy is envisaged in respect of social services and education, in the areas to which they are to be confined. They will have no say in

---

[1] Under an amendment of 1961, some of those removed have been permitted temporarily to retain their shops.

[2] Already there is apparent evidence of impoverishment in some parts.

justice or the determination of the bulk of the laws of the Republic which they will have to obey.

The lessons are, it seems to me, indisputable. Even if the Indians had had the right to political representation on the basis of 'one man one vote', they would still have been a mere minority, and as such they could have expected little consideration from so-called democratic governments.[1] For in these days it is believed to be defensible for the politically powerful to serve their interest at the expense of the politically weak. In contrast, the market is always impersonal, disinterested and neutral. When the state is equally impartial, the market solution to the problems of access to opportunity and income distribution would satisfy the ordinary man's criteria of equity; and even when (through lack of constitutional limitations on governmental power) the state panders to political privilege, the whole force of the free market is exerted in opposition to it.

---

[1] Unless they could have determined the balance between roughly equal political parties.

CHAPTER 15

THE DIRECTION OF AFRICAN LABOUR

ONE OF the most curious aspects of the political situation in South Africa is the fact that a government which has passed an Act for the Suppression of Communism, aimed mainly at eradicating the activities of the Communist Party or Communist fellow-travellers among the Africans, has itself imposed a more or less authoritarian system on them. The effects of the policies described in this Chapter have been to create controls which bear a close resemblance to the system of labour allocation found behind the Iron Curtain.

THE 'PASS LAWS'
A useful tool in this control has been a document of identification known as a 'pass' (officially called a 'reference book'). Since the pass is proof of poll tax payment as well as of identification, the duty to carry it ought not to have become a source of bitterness.[1] It happens, however, that African resentment has come to be more strongly felt against these Pass laws than against other laws which have been even more effective in withholding opportunities from them.

The reason appears to be that the penalties imposed on Africans who have been unable to produce their passes on demand have been extremely heavy, and their frequent inability to pay the fines has resulted in an enormous number of jail sentences for mere petty negligence. The general administration of these laws appears to have been harsh rather than precise. The rank and file of the police, who have the task of calling upon Africans to show their passes, have reflected the traditional Afrikaner outlook towards colour and have carried out their duties with crude severity, so that Africans have often been roughly addressed and

---
[1] The 'Pass Laws', originally applying to slaves and hottentots, date from the days of the East India Company. In the case of the large number of foreign migrant Africans who find employment in South Africa, the 'pass' has really served as a passport. Foreign Africans are now to be required to carry proper passports.

even roughly handled by them. That is one reason why the Pass laws have engendered feelings of burning injustice and earned the enmity of Africans as a whole. Moreover, the prodigious number of charges brought under these laws seems to have encouraged many over-worked magistrates to deal out rugged rather than considered justice.[1]

A further cause of bitterness among the better educated Africans is that they are often peremptorily called upon to show their passes by poorly educated white police who all too often regard the cultured speech and bearing of well-educated Africans as arrogance. If they have inadvertently forgotten to carry their passes, they are likely to be subjected to the grossest humiliation.

But the chief cause for the hostility of Africans to these laws of recent years seems to be that they have become part of the apparatus through which the black races have been cut off from potential opportunities of employment. Business men and industrialists seeking profits through cheap labour have been straining to offer what have appeared to Africans as well-paid opportunities. But the latter have been increasingly forbidden to accept such offers by official decision and directed to other types of work.

PLANNING BY 'INFLUX CONTROL'

The controls have been exercised until recently mainly under

---

[1] For instance, Dr Helen Suzman, MP, referred recently to the enormous number of pass law cases in which sentences ranged from £7 10s. or 15 days' imprisonment to £45 or 90 days, and African youths were sentenced to up to 8 cuts. She said: 'I am not against corporal punishment *per se*. I can see that it has a use against thugs who go around assaulting people ... But I cannot by any stretch of the imagination see why cuts have to be imposed on youths for statutory offences'. She went on to say, from personal observation at certain Bantu Commissioners Courts, that the sittings reminded her of a sausage machine. 'Hundreds of Africans came up in Court ... it takes 2 minutes to have the whole matter interpreted and dealt with and the verdict is R10 or ten days, or R20 or twenty days. [R2 equals £1.] So it goes on over and over again'. The Minister replied that there was a group of young Africans who banded together in a campaign not to carry their passes and that their parents had asked that they should be caned.

At the Bantu Commissioners Court at Port Elizabeth 316 men and 47 women were sentenced, over a period of 9 weeks, to a total of £5,500 in fines or 13,000 days imprisonment, and 74 youths and 24 young men received a total of 640 cuts.

what is now called 'influx control'. In 1923, previous municipal regulations applying to Africans were strengthened, extended and standardised by a measure of central control enacted through the Native (Urban Areas) Act. The chief aim of this Act was (or at any rate was represented to be) the improvement of the conditions of African urban residence. There was, of course, need for some such legislation, just as there is for municipal regulation everywhere; and there were fears that the truly appalling conditions which had been allowed to develop in some locations had contributed to the severity of a disastrous influenza epidemic of 1918. The failure of the 1923 legislation to prevent the continuance or emergence of slum or semi-slum conditions in the locations of many towns was chiefly due, I think, not to defects in the Act under discussion, but indirectly to other laws which prevented Africans from acquiring skills, particularly in building. Had the black people been freely allowed to serve their own community (even if not the Whites and Coloureds), entrepreneurs would have seen to it that the urban services needed to eliminate slum conditions (roads, sanitation, water, and houses instead of shanties) were provided at a wage-cost which the beneficiaries could have afforded.[1]

The Native (Urban Areas) Act was, however, undoubt-

---

[1] Concern with world opinion about the condition under which urban Africans (outside the mining compounds) were living appears to have been mainly responsible (a) for the relaxation in 1951 of the prohibition on the training and employment of Africans as building artisans (see Chapter 10, p. 95), and (b) for the introduction in 1952 of the 'Native Services Levy', a sort of local poll tax paid by employers for each African employed (other than as domestic servants or on farms). The proceeds of the levy have been used to provide, in the urban locations, the sort of services which are paid for by local rates in most municipal areas: street lighting, sewage, roads, refuse collection, etc. A later Act imposed a Transport Levy (also on employers) to subsidise the cost of Africans travelling to and from employment. This was necessary because they had been, in many cases, forced to reside at long distances from their places of employment.

The provision of these services by such means is believed by many to have militated against the interests of Africans; first, by causing recourse to labour-economising methods of a kind which have not been allowed to have their normal effect of engendering alternative employments for those displaced; and second, by encouraging employers to substitute other forms of non-white labour for African labour.

edly used not only to regulate the influx to the towns, but (after the Second World War) to discourage or prevent Africans from making full use of the opportunities for material and social advancement which the free market was offering.[1] In 1945, the machinery of prohibitions, permits and exemptions was developed in detail. Since then every employer of an African in industry or commerce has been required to register each wage contract individually. Every African is required to obtain a permit to be in any urban area and produce it on demand (in addition to having to produce his pass or 'reference book'). An employed African is not allowed to change his employment without official sanction (easily obtainable before 1952). Moreover, the Government was accorded complete discretion to refuse permission to any African woman to take up employment or residence in any urban area. But since the Native Laws Amendment Act of 1952, the Africans have been increasingly subject to a totalitarian form of official control and regimentation. As might have been expected, the avowed purpose of this Act is 'economic planning' to eliminate the 'waste' of African labour through its 'uneconomic employment'. The assumption is that officials know better than the market what the African labour 'requirements' of each area are and are able to ensure that the African labour supply is 'properly' allocated. All the typically totalitarian paraphernalia of central, regional, district and local African labour bureaux was created in 1952, and elaborated in a Bill introduced in 1963, to supersede the market by outright direction of African labour.

ECONOMIC CASE AGAINST 'INFLUX CONTROL'

Yet throughout the implementation of the different influx control acts, industrialists have been trying to circumvent their provisions. The fight has taken the form partly of attempting to evade the obvious intentions, but partly of begging for permission to offer employment. Since the advent of the Nationalist Government (in 1948), however,

---

[1] Additional aims of the 1923 Act, and subsequent influx control legislation (in principle defensible in the light of liberal ideals), were to facilitate the working of the Masters' and Servants' Acts (see Chapter 10, pp. 92-3) and to control liquor (including Kaffir beer).

resistance from industrialists has seldom taken the form of political opposition to the influx control laws; for open opposition in the political sphere from individuals might well mean the loss of the many favours which a government armed with authoritarian powers of control can hand out. The industrialists' resistance was based on recognition that the community wanted and would always demand the products which African labour could provide, and took the form of dodging state-imposed restraints. Had the legal obstacles to making the best use of African labour been less formidable, managements might indeed have been induced (in the course of profit-seeking) to provide not merely employment opportunities for Africans but education and an environment conducive to industrial efficiency[1] such as a normal family life. But here again the interests of investors have clashed with government policies.

With few exceptions the Republic official regards all Africans as merely standard 'put and carry' workers; and since 1952 very little freedom of choice seems to have been permitted to managements in recruiting this class of labour. Employers have been forced to choose the best they could from those permitted, by the bureaucracy, to join the pool of registered work-seekers in any district. The resulting waste of human powers and destruction of employee incentives must have been considerable; for even under the restricted opportunities for education and skill permitted by collectivist policies, African employees differ from one another in physical strength, eyesight, manual dexterity, literacy, *savoir faire*, reliability and experience. Hence the loss in productivity arising from official direction of labour is probably far larger than most industrialists realise.

The African himself is as dependent upon the whim of the politicians and officials as he would be in a totalitarian country. He has to receive permission not only to enter a

---

[1] I must repeat that I am not claiming that altruistic motives would have actuated such developments. For instance, continuous improvements in respect of miners' diets, sporting and general recreation facilities, standards of compound accommodation and medical and hospital services on the mines were accelerated by the competition of industrial occupations, which were attracting Africans from the mines. The steps taken to meet this competition were not disinterested. None the less they were laudable and enlightened.

particular urban area but to leave any area in which he lives. He may be given permission (in his reference book) to work only in a particular district, in a particular industry, in a particular type of work, or even for one particular employer. And in practice, if he has lost one town job, he is virtually compelled to accept any other employment offered to him. If he does not, he runs the risk of being 'endorsed out' of the urban area in which he has been working. Formerly an African had the right to continue to live and work in any area in which he had been born or in which he had been employed for ten years or more. Since 1952, he has no longer had that right. He may be removed by the Minister and permitted then to work (outside his 'homeland') only where the Department of Bantu Administration decides. Indeed, at the caprice of an official, or on a Minister's decree, an African may be shifted from one area to another; diverted from one employment or occupation to another; and even removed, with little concern for human feelings or any resulting delinquency and illegitimacy, from his wife and family. He has no right of appeal to the Courts. It is not difficult to imagine the sense of helplessness and insecurity which the urban African must experience.

TOWARDS APARTHEID

The latest legislation, introduced in 1963, is intended to implement this policy by codifying 11 previous Acts and carrying further the enforcement of segregation wherever Whites and non-Whites have to co-operate in economic activity. It does so by reinforcing the power of official regimentation. Under the Bantu Laws Amendment Bill (which is expected to become law in 1964 and which has given rise to grave – although little publicly expressed – disquiet among industrialists), the Minister of Bantu Administration and Development will become the supreme director of initiative in the industrial and commercial spheres. He will be accorded dictatorial powers over the use of African labour. Thus, he will be able to determine the areas from which Africans may be recruited; the number of Africans who may be employed in any defined area; the location of industries in which they may be employed; and the specific employers for whom they may work. He will have the right to compel Africans who are displaced from jobs (so that their work shall be done by other races) to move to depots from which they will be allocated to labour camps, unless they happen to be migratory labourers who can be returned to the reserves. The Minister will also have the right – delegated to an official in one of the labour bureaux – to detain in depots adult Africans who are unemployed or who refuse any job offered to them[1] or who are convicted (without Court trial but by administrative process) of breaches of the pass laws, influx control regulations and Native Labour regulations. Further powers include the right to detain unemployed Africans under 21 in youth camps; and even to remove from a particular area Africans born in it or who have lived in it for long periods,[2] provided they are declared 'surplus labour' or 'redundant' or 'idle' or 'undesirable' or provided that, in the Minister's opinion, it is 'in the public interest' that they shall be removed.[3]

If the Bill is passed no African will be allowed to work outside the reserves except as an employee of a white-owned company or person (otherwise than through special permission) and the self-employment of Africans will be virtually forbidden. Every contract of service with an African worker will henceforth have to be registered officially; heavier penalties will be imposed for employing an African without a permit; and no African will be allowed to live in a rural area outside a reserve or outside a 'Bantustan' unless he is employed by the owner of the land or is a labour tenant or squatter.

Not the least serious aspect of this Bill is the scope for

---

[1]This provision might seem to make unemployment a crime.
[2]Those in this category will, however, have the privilege of being the last to be expelled.
[3]Outspoken criticism of the first draft of the Bill resulted in the concession (if it can be really so termed) that, in the implementation of such transfer, the authorities 'must take into consideration the Bantu's family ties and other commitments', and that there must be 'suitable other work' (in the opinion of politicians or officials) for him to go to. Incidentally the Minister of Bantu Administration will acquire virtually absolute power to determine the future siting of industry; for there is hardly a single industry which does not employ more African labour than White or Coloured labour.

corruption which it will create. 'At every essential point', commented the *Cape Times* during the debates on the measure, 'the decision is in the right of an underpaid official, without possibility of proper supervision and without the machinery of publicity and court proceedings with which intelligent communities protect themselves from subversion by bribery.'

A major aim appears to be the deliberate destruction of such family life as the Africans have retained in the urban areas and the discouragement of Africans from sharing in Western culture (which means, incidentally, from sharing in Western values).[1]

The justification always put forward for these policies is that the Africans are, properly considered, merely temporary visitors to the areas in which they are employed. But as the *Cape Times* cogently explained recently, we are naming as 'temporary sojourners' or aliens 'the very people on whose labour our wealth depends', whilst 'these terms are used of people who help us rear our children, serve us with food in hotels, teach in Western type schools and even lecture in our universities'.

The administrative cost of all these controls is growing annually mainly because of the increasing difficulty of maintaining law and order (whether owing to the resentments aroused or the mounting influence of African nationalism). But in part the cost arises out of the necessity to appease world opinion by providing 'separate facilities'. Another, so far smaller, expense has been the purchase of support for *apartheid* from chiefs[2] and other non-white leaders. Whereas in 1948 (just before the introduction of *apartheid*) the Department of Native Affairs had an annual budget of under £3.5 million and a staff of 185, in 1962 its successor, the Department of Bantu Administration and Development, already had a budget of nearly £13.5 million and a staff of 735.

---

[1] The fact that state-provided education for African children, controlled by the Department of Bantu Education, is now restricted to Standard II (except within the Africans' 'homelands', where higher education of a type, also government controlled, is available), is relevant to this thesis.
[2] In 1962, the sum of £146,000 was allocated under the heading 'Allowances, Presents and Rations to Chiefs and Headmen'.

If these multiplying expenditures could be shown to have been to the advantage of the Africans controlled they could be justified. But they appear to have been used mainly in the suppression of discontent and the wasteful duplication of 'separate' services.

ABANDONMENT OF THE RULE OF LAW

The methods employed to prevent subversion and disorder are also based on the totalitarian model. The rule of law has been abandoned, so that those who are suspected of trouble-making may be deprived of their liberty (by being subjected to house arrest, confined to particular areas or detained *incommunicado* for 90 days for 'questioning') without normal court processes. The principle that no person shall be punished unless judicial procedures have established the breach of some clear-cut law no longer applies. The fate of an alleged offender is determined not by a judge or a jury but by a politician or, under the '90 days' rule, by a police officer.

It is not necessary to my argument to assume that these powers have been abused or that there is any intention to abuse them. The weakness in the judicial process of the free society is that its satisfactory functioning may sometimes be defeated by unscrupulous stratagems,[1] which the Pan-Africans have learned. The Communists, however, and their saboteur trainees in South Africa, are not attempting to subvert a free society. They are trying to undermine a country which may be regarded as free for the Whites alone, and even for the Whites in certain senses only. In the old Transvaal and Free State Republics, and since 1910 in South Africa, the non-Whites have never experienced what the educated among them could be expected to regard as justice or, indeed, the conditions of freedom, in either the

---

[1] To take a parallel case, the surviving power of gangsterdom in the United States could undoubtedly be broken most easily if the administration there had the power to apprehend 'known' (i.e., suspected) gangsters and incarcerate them without trial. But in spite of the magnitude of the gangster evil, any temptation to use such methods has been wisely restrained; for it would be, in effect, conferring arbitrary power on politicians and destroying confidence in the administration of justice. Most Americans realise that the influence of the gangsters will ultimately be terminated through the normal process of law in the Courts.

economic or political spheres. Injustice is the food on which the communist type of trouble-maker thrives. The paradox of South Africa is that the proponents of *apartheid* are, on the one hand, feeding the subversionists and on the other hand trying to suppress them.

It is this situation which creates the cruel dilemma of the true South African liberals. They must support action, even drastic action, to counteract a form of subversive activity which exploits violence and relies on the intimidation of non-conforming Africans by threats of murder and bodily harm. But when the defenders of intellectual and economic freedom approve of the only procedures which many believe can be effective to suppress subversion, they seem to be defending the very policies which have played into the hands of the would-be saboteurs.

It is, however, in the nature of extreme collectivist administrations that they welcome arbitrary powers; and it is perhaps for that reason that the methods adopted by the Government of the Republic have come to resemble so closely those of the countries behind the Iron Curtain. I hope it is not wishful thinking on my part when I record my belief that a truly democratic society, i.e., a liberal society, could resist the assaults of Communist-type intrigues without the crude injustices of administrative jurisdiction.[1]

It is difficult to imagine a better illustration than is provided by South Africa of the truth that the fight against colour injustice is actually against the consequences of planning on the collectivist model. Every repression of the

---

[1] One factor which encourages the shrewd Nationalist politicians of the Republic and discourages their liberal critics is that the former know only too well that the ruthless suppression of discontent is hardly likely to bring greater opprobrium than the almost opposite policy. Thus, in the British South African Protectorates, African nationalism has almost completely free rein, including the right to complain to the world of 'oppression', the right to organise to throw off 'the British yoke', and even the right to receive funds from Ghana for this purpose! As a special correspondent in *The Times* has recently expressed it, 'the bitterest lesson for the British' is that, in the eyes of the non-white world, they are 'indistinguishable from the South Africans as oppressors of the black man'. *The Times*, 3 January, 1963.

Africans has, at the same time, been a repression of the free market. It is so-called 'central planning' which has caused African labour to become regarded as a mere source of useful, unskilled, muscular strength. And it is profit incentives which have tended powerfully to raise the material standards of Africans, to develop their latent powers, to raise their status and prestige in a multi-racial society, and ultimately to win for them equality of respect and consideration.

Not only has the centralisation of economic power through the Native Law Amendment Act and similarly orientated legislation prevented investment in Africans as human capital; it has substituted for the delicate and sensitive co-ordination effected by responsible decision-makers – subject to the disciplines of the loss-avoidance incentives – the decisions of officials controlled by no such impartial disciplines. Officials are irresponsible in respect of the social sanctions of the market, absolved from any profit or loss test of achievement, accountable merely to politicians, and subject to the temptation of corruption. Of course, politicians are responsible to electorates. But electors are much less rational and well-informed than consumers.

The Africans, of whom about two-thirds are forced to work outside any conceivable reserve 'Bantustan' of the future,[1] have been left with no more civil rights than they would have as labourers in totalitarian countries. Their lives have become almost wholly regimented by officials whose decisions cannot be legally challenged. Because they, the Africans, have no voice whatsoever in the choice of the government, they are placed in the same position as any other political 'minority' under 'omnipotent representative government'.

I contrast 'omnipotent government' with what some Americans are beginning to call the 'libertarian' tradition (because the socialists have taken to describing themselves as 'liberal') but which I still prefer to call 'liberal'. Under the liberal tradition, the powers of governments are restrained by rigid constitutional entrenchments which (i) protect minorities from spoliation by majorities, (ii) guaran-

---

[1] See Chapter 17.

tee the independence of the judiciary,[1] and (iii) prohibit delegated legislation (unless subject to immediate and effective parliamentary review) and administrative jurisdiction.

PRESSURES ON EMPLOYERS

It may be asked why, if the private enterprise system is opposed to *apartheid*, investors and managements have not used their financial and political power to prevent it? The answer is that, as in the United States, Britain and other countries in the Western world, investors and managers are a political minority. Apart from the pressures on them to maintain 'good industrial relations' by appeasing white employees, they are all too often inhibited from openly or effectively criticising a policy which is against their long-term interest because they fear the state. For instance, in the sphere we have been discussing, private undertakings are at the mercy of officials (nominally, the Minister of Bantu Administration) concerning the amount of African labour they are allowed to employ. Is it surprising that directors and managers have tended to become servile to the Government? An open opponent of *apartheid* may well fear, *inter alia*, that his competitor will be quietly allowed plenty of African labour whilst he is allowed little. He will have no appeal to the Courts. And the Government have not hesitated to remind business men of the big stick which the centralisation of economic power enables them to wield. For instance, the Minister of Bantu Administration recently warned those white traders of the Transkei who had been criticising the Bantustan proposals (see Chapter 17), which appeared to threaten them with ruin, that 'if it had to depend on him, they would have no reason to expect anything from him when the time came'.[2] It is significant that the Transkei Territories Civic Association, pointing out that 'the threat by the Minister savours of intimidation', pleaded that they did not have the wrong opinions; that they were not guilty of taking part in politics; that they were 'not

---

[1]The traditions of judicial independence, within the diminished sphere left to the Courts, appear so far to have survived in South Africa, in spite of the suspicion that some appointments to the bench have been politically motivated.
[2]*Argus*, 6 March, 1963.

agitators'; and therefore that the Minister's threat was unjustified. They seemed almost to take for granted his right to damage those who take the wrong line in politics.

Some business men have told me that their reluctance publicly to criticise the present government is due less to fear of arbitrary ministerial or official action than the threat of organised boycotts through quiet ministerial suggestions to provincial and local administrations and to powerful Afrikaner business organisations subject to party discipline. Indeed, they feel that, in the interests of their investors and employees, they are compelled occasionally to make public gestures of approval of the ruling party, although a longer view of their interests might prompt frank opposition. The extent to which would-be critics of the Government do, in fact, fear reprisals is illustrated by the recent appeal of the huge Bristol-Myers Co. to the Cabinet, asking that they should be declared innocent of the charge of intentionally sponsoring a biased TV film about South Africa called 'Sabotage'.

There is no way, I suggest, of ever preventing such abuse of state power except 'liberal' constitutional entrenchments which limit the sphere of parliaments to the enactment of non-discriminatory laws, and limit the powers of cabinets to the initiation and non-discriminatory execution of those laws. Such constitutional restraints would prohibit the political direction of labour and economic activity generally. It implies, therefore, the acceptance of the only alternative form of co-ordination, namely the social discipline of the free market in a legal framework designed to avoid the concentration or abuse of power by exposing all owners of resources or suppliers of goods or services to open competition in meeting the wishes of the sovereign consumer. And that discipline is exerted through permitting politically unrestrained investment in human capital and the attraction of labour to where its contribution to the common pool of output, and hence its value, is largest.

CHAPTER 16

THE BORDER AREAS

IN pursuit of the objectives of *apartheid* or separate development, the proclaimed policy of the Nationalist Government has, since 1955, been (a) to establish 'border industries' near the reserves where it is assumed that Africans can be more suitably employed as labourers by white capitalists in integrated co-operation with white artisans and supervisors; and (b) to establish 'Bantustans', i.e., districts from which white capitalists (and ultimately white supervisors and artisans) will be excluded, but in which Africans will be allowed some considerable measure of local autonomy and 'ultimate independence'.[1]

In 1921, the Stallard Commission had recommended that Blacks should not be allowed in white areas except as temporary employees. By then a relatively small number had become resident in white districts (excluding farming and mining areas). But since that time the great African influx into industry has created a situation which can, I believe, never be reversed. The slow influx of Africans during the 1920s was accelerated after 1934 by the stimulus of an increased dollar price of gold, and later by the acute labour scarcity of the Second World War. The 15 years of *apartheid* policy since 1948 have so far resulted in no discernible deceleration. Far from any net return of Africans to their presently defined 'homelands', we may more reasonably expect a net exodus.

FORCES WORKING AGAINST APARTHEID
The inescapable truth is that, over the decade up to 1961, in spite of influx control and the extraordinarily drastic Native Laws Amendment Act of 1951, a million additional Africans were attracted to employment in soundly located

---
[1] The latter project is discussed in Chapter 17.

activities which are mostly far from the border areas;[1] and the total number of urban Africans in the whole country, which increased by nearly 50 per cent between 1951 and 1960 (from 2.3 million to 3.4 million), is likely to continue to grow, even if part of the growth occurs in the border areas. Indeed the larger probability is of a slowly increasing trek of African labour away from the reserves or Bantustans and from the farms to the existing urban areas or areas adjacent to them. The number of adult male Africans living in the reserves or Bantustans may then form a declining proportion of their total numbers. But of course reckless 'endorsement out' of politically selected regions or occupations may well reduce local African populations.[2]

Statistics of employment in industry by race show remarkable consistency over the years. The trends have hardly been disturbed during the 15 years of *apartheid* policy, in spite of increasingly drastic enforcement intended to reverse them. This suggests that even harsher recourse to methods which we usually associate with the administration of Soviet communities, as in the Bantu Laws Amendment Bill, will be no more successful. I cannot help thinking that the politicians responsible, having been concerned almost entirely with the effects of their proposals upon electoral, United Nations and International Court approval, have never applied their minds to the significance of the statistical history of the last 40 years.[3]

---

[1] In the first half of 1963, the Government's own labour bureau recruited more Africans from the Transkei than in any of the previous three years, and mostly from the Western Cape. Moreover, as this is being written, the state railways are employing a record number of Africans.

[2] For instance, presumably through efforts to remove Africans from the Western Cape, in the five chief municipal areas of the Cape Province the non-white population grew by only 36 per cent from 1951 to 1960 (as against the 50 per cent for all urban areas). But the number of African workers in industry as a whole increased by 41 per cent (as against a 26 per cent increase in the number of white workers).

[3] I am confirmed in this opinion by reason of the surprising lack of familiarity with the official statistics relevant to his department shown recently by the Deputy Minister of Economic Affairs (see my letter in the *Cape Times* of 5 April, 1963, the Deputy Minister's reply on 11 April, 1963, and my rejoinder on 19 April, 1963), and some absurd claims about the statistical implications of border industries development which have been made by the Prime Minister (see letters from Dr S. van der Horst, *Cape Times*, 9 April, 1963, and *Cape Argus*, 25 April, 1963).

Nevertheless, the announced objective is slowly to remove African labour from certain established industrial areas. With this end in view, the Government is not only diverting Africans (by influx control) from these regions but giving conspicuous, much publicised, yet so far not very effective special encouragement[1] for the 'border industries'. The announced intention is that, as elsewhere, the more highly skilled and responsible work shall continue to be undertaken by Whites. Hence the aim is the perpetuation of a form of economic integration but the transfer of this integration to what are regarded as more appropriate districts. But unless the African employees to be moved by authority are to be forced into farm or mine work, they will have to find jobs in as yet non-existent industries, in what are now agricultural districts; and with the exception of certain areas near East London, Durban, Maritzburg, Newcastle and west of Pretoria,[2] the border areas intended are almost as poorly located as the projected Bantustans. They are mostly far removed from sources of materials and markets for potential products; they have hardly any water schemes, extremely backward transport arrangements, and inadequate power supplies; and they lack near-by mining industry which might render profitable the establishment of service industries and complementary industries. The border activities will, however, benefit from specially generous financial assistance through the state-operated Industrial Development Corporation,[3] from special allowances to industrialists under the Income Tax Act of 1961, from wage-rate concessions,[4] from special railway rates (at present rather uncertain), from the provision on favourable terms (i.e., at the taxpayers' expense) of transport, water,

---

[1] The Prime Minister has recently admitted that the progress of border industries has been slow, but he claims that it is gaining pace.
[2] These areas were (partly by reason of access to raw materials) destined to attract industries in any case. Indeed, in my judgment they would, on the whole, have progressed industrially more rapidly under the prosperity likely in the absence of *apartheid*. They might be termed the 'pseudo-border areas'. It is not clear why the economic integration of Blacks and Whites is to be welcomed in, say, the Pretoria district but not in the Cape Town district.
[3] Including the leasing of factories at heavily subsidised rentals.
[4] In wage-board determinations and in extensions to the border areas of industrial council agreements.

sewage, effluent disposal and power, probably from preferential tariff treatment, and finally from various unpublicised favours promised to promoters. A number of factories have been established in the border areas, presumably through quiet ministerial assurances that these special competitive advantages (which burden the taxpayer with a heavy capital cost for every border employee) will be perpetuated for some time.

ECONOMIC BURDEN OF APARTHEID

Now for many years I have been teaching my students what seem to be the lessons of recorded experience that the most vital entrepreneurial decision – which can make all the difference between the success or failure of a new enterprise – is that relating to its location. I have always accepted that the best measure of centralisation or decentralisation of industrial activity (and other economic operations) in any area is likely to be achieved when the decisions are made on behalf of those who risk large capital sums in the development;[1] and I have always regarded it as one of the major weaknesses of state control that political objectives are only too likely to dominate the issue, because officials and politicians are not themselves personally responsible for losses and do not bear the consequences.[2]

But government spokesmen have made surprisingly optimistic forecasts of the numbers of Africans whom they hope to be able to direct or attract, without disaster, away from where they are at present contributing to output, to segregated integration in new areas. If they do succeed in transferring large numbers in this way, it will be almost entirely through the operation of differential wage-rates, which are very much lower in the border industries than in the already established industrial areas, with hours of labour longer and fringe benefits (including overtime payments) considerably

---

[1] Much of the talk about the need for centralisation of industry emanates from a doctrinaire belief that the centralisation of industrial activity, which has led to the growth of towns, has for some reason been uneconomic. But such concentration has been the consequence of the decisions of those who have stood to gain from wise decisions and to bear heavy losses when their forecasts have turned out to be wrong.

[2] This is evidenced in South Africa in such things as the enormous mileage of uneconomically provided branch railway lines.

less generous. The *Financial Mail* complained recently that in the clothing industry African wage-rates were 28 per cent lower in border areas than in Durban (where, on the whole, African wage-rates in the established industrial area are lowest).

> 'The gap is often enormous, and while border theorists emphasise wage differentiation they are really defending a low wage policy.'

If such wage-rate discrepancies were merely sufficient to off-set the longer distances of the established industrial areas from the reserves and the larger social costs to Africans of being forced to live so far from wives and families, no injustices would be caused by the differentiation. Indeed, at relatively low wage-rates African labour could (irrespective of any other 'subsidy' element) be bid away from areas such as the Western Cape and the Rand. But industrialists who have started in the border areas seem to regard all the other special advantages as chicken feed in comparison with the lower labour costs they have been promised. If this opinion is justified, it follows that disparities in labour cost must be caused by the exclusion of Africans (by means of influx control and 'endorsing out') from the established areas to which they would otherwise be attracted. The *Financial Mail* has described the border districts as 'local Hong Kongs'. But the labour of Hong Kong is cheap because distance and immigration laws prevent its people from moving to areas where their productivity would be higher; whilst in the case of border areas, African labour is cheap because it is being deliberately excluded or driven from the regions in which its contribution to the common pool of output has been larger.

It seems probable that many border industries will survive only if Africans employed in the new industrial areas are quietly permitted to undertake far more skilled and productive tasks than in the established industrial areas (from which they are to be withdrawn or withheld in future). Otherwise their survival will demand even bigger preferential advantages or subsidies than are already being offered. There was no hint of such a policy when the scheme was first put forward. But just as the final revision of this book was being made, the Prime Minister made a statement[1] referring to 'measures being taken' to provide 'more and better employment opportunities for Coloured people and Indians and for trained and unskilled Bantu (Africans) in the Bantu homeland areas and the border area industries'.[2] If this means that Africans are to be allowed to undertake skilled work in the border regions it is an oblique announcement of a remarkable breach in the economic *apartheid* dyke. But it will be grossly unjust to the pioneer industrial regions.

Outside government circles, however, few have had much faith in the possibility of a large number of Africans ever finding employment in the true border areas.[3] There are many critics who fear that the claimed objective is merely window-dressing for the benefit of the outside world and that there is no real intention to persevere with it. Others regard it as a manoeuvre to acquire cheap labour for the farms and mines. What will in fact take place, says one responsible critic,[4]

> 'is wholesale removal of African families to the congested and underdeveloped African areas, where there neither is nor can be employment or land available for their support. There they will be dumped in "rural villages" under conditions of destitution that will force the men to accept employment as migrant labourers on farms, mines and so on, on such terms as may be offered to them through the District Labour Bureaux'.

At times it seems to be admitted that a distortion of the location of industry must be accepted as part of a courageous economic sacrifice needed for the political and sociological

---

[1] *Cape Times*, 4 October, 1963.

[2] Whilst this book was in the press the Minister of Labour was more explicit. He announced in the Senate (13 February, 1964) that there would be no ceiling to the skills Africans could acquire in the border areas.

[3] As distinct from certain areas near the reserves which were, in any case, destined to develop industrially. In the last year for which the Industrial Development Corporation has reported, an additional 1,850 Africans obtained employment in border industries out of 400,000 employed in industry as a whole. The IDC is a state-financed body which assists the financing of industry and has been instructed to do everything possible to develop the border areas.

[4] Donald Molteno, QC, a leading constitutional authority and member of the Progressive Party, *Cape Times*, 10 March, 1963.

advantages of separate development. Thus, the diversion of industrial integration to new districts appears sometimes to be demanding that favourably located areas, such as the Western Cape, must acquiesce in damage both from labour shortage and from privileged development in poorly-located districts. But the Government has fought shy of calling upon the community as a whole (the supposed beneficiaries) to pay directly for these advantages through open subsidies to border industries. By such open transfers, everybody would have known what the border industries were costing the community in taxation. Similarly, if the plan had set up state-owned 'border' industries, the public would at least have known the annual losses (or profits) from the investment. The Prime Minister has claimed, however, that the South African economy is founded on the principle of private initiative, and that state-owned activity would violate that principle.[1]

CONTRADICTIONS, EVASIONS, AND CONSEQUENCES

At other times it is argued that there will be no damage to existing industrial areas (e.g., the Western Cape) which, although they will in due course lose their traditional form of unskilled labour, will be relieved from 'over-employment'; or that mechanisation, or the substitution of the labour of Whites or Coloureds, will rectify any labour scarcity; or that established industries will not be allowed to suffer from under-cutting in the sale of output from the privileged areas;[2] or that the process will be so gradual that no disruption will occur. The assurance of the present chairman of the Board of Trade and Industries that any special 'assistance' accorded these areas will not be 'unfair', because

---

[1] One can understand the Government's unwillingness for these economic activities either to show a loss or be blamed for 'unfair' competition with old established industrial areas. But one can hardly describe as 'private enterprise' a system under which, before any industrialist can contemplate the inauguration of any large-scale industry, he must first consult government departments and Ministers to find out where he may locate the development in order to escape penalties or enjoy privileges which can make the difference between success and failure.

[2] E.g., cotton and rayon textiles to be segregated in the border areas and woollen or nylon textiles to be permitted to continue in existing areas.

the developments fostered will be 'on a complementary basis and not competitive',[1] is hardly convincing. For even if the form of investment in 'border' development is determined, not by assessments of profitability but according to the extent to which it is believed the projected output will not compete with existing kinds of output in the Republic, the new factories will still be competing for the scarce resources of the community.

There is much evidence that the policy has never been carefully thought out. Thus, although ministers have hinted at the possibility of white people having to do without black domestic service, to which household economies have been adjusted in many parts of South Africa, householders have been assured that they will not be robbed of their African servants.[2] As the *Cape Times* remarked:

> 'if the Government told the country flatly that for the sake of separate development housewives must make do without servants, like the vast majority of their sisters in Europe, the United States and Australia . . . we would have vastly more respect for the Government's sincerity about separate development. It would then be possible to believe the implications of *apartheid* were actually being faced.'

The Western Cape has been chosen as a guinea-pig area, in which the Government can seek to prove that it is practicable, without disaster to the Whites, to dispense with African labour. Yet it is here that wage-rates for unskilled work (which reflect marginal productivity) are the highest in the country. Does this not suggest that African labour has become vital for the continued prosperity of the area.[3] Possibly the Western Cape has been chosen because it is politically the least powerful, returning relatively few

---

[1] Apparently, therefore, the intention is that the new industries shall enjoy just sufficient privilege to off-set their locational disadvantages.
[2] But in the future only one African servant will be permitted to live in without a special permit.
[3] Already by the 1880s, considerable numbers had been attracted to the Western Cape for labouring work; and shortly after the Boer War it became expedient, mainly for public health reasons, to provide a location for them at Ndabeni. During the present century, the influx continued slowly until the First World War, when the growing African population began to give rise to misgivings. But since 1934 the number

Nationalist members to Parliament.[1] To those who object that the economic growth of this area is to be restrained for the benefit of, say, the Pretoria region, the Minister replies that such critics put a little economic growth before a matter of great principle. But industrial progress in the Western Cape has already been lagging for some time behind the other main industrial areas of the Republic, due I believe mainly to stricter enforcement of influx control plus 'endorsement out'. From the beginning of 1959 until April, 1962, about 26,000 Africans (of whom 7,000 were women) were 'endorsed out' of the Western Cape against their will, and only a small proportion are likely yet to have found employment in the reserves or border areas. Some will probably be working on farms, in other established industrial regions, or in the mines; and some will be virtually unemployed – which is quite unusual for Africans.[2]

Worried industrialists and farmers have been assured that the removal of Africans will be gradual because, in the meantime, their labour is still needed by the white man. It will take place, they are told, without disruption of industry and over a long period. But if the Blacks are told that, although they are needed now in, say, the Western Cape, in the long run they must regard themselves as unwanted there, feelings of insecurity, resentment and even desperation must result. Some commentators have suggested – not without plausibility – that the threat of 'endorsement out' had been a major cause of the emergence of the Poqo organisation (relying upon violent resistance) which, apparently, originated in the Western Cape.

Despite government denials, it is really not unreasonable to infer that only the deepest sense of injustice could have induced the sudden change of attitude during the last

---

employed in the Western Cape has grown by more than five times. Today, over 180,000 find employment in this area where they make up about one-eighth of the population, about 40 per cent of them being in rural areas and 60 per cent in urban areas.

[1] The Western Cape envisaged is the area west of a line running from Humansdorp through Pearston, Middelburg, Colesburg, Hopetown, Prieska and Namaqualand.

[2] See Chapter 10, pp. 95–6.

decade by urban Africans who had formerly been happy, smiling, patient, submissive, respectful and courteous in their dealings with Whites.[1] No doubt trouble-making agitators have played a role; but they have always been active, and we should be asking ourselves why they have suddenly had so much success in recent years. The causes of the new unrest, which have goaded the Government into the most extreme forms of repression, can hardly be unconnected with the administration of doctrinaire *apartheid*.

It has been claimed for the border industries policy that the proximity of the border regions to the reserves will ameliorate the admittedly unsatisfactory sociological conditions under which urban Africans have so far had to live. Certainly some of them will be able to visit their families over week-ends or, at any rate, over long week-ends; and it may well be possible to provide better living quarters and amenities. Otherwise, nearness to the reserves or the Bantustans is hardly likely to cause material improvement. Of course, if Africans were allowed to bring their wives and families to the border areas, it would mean an enormously important compensating advantage. But that is definitely not what is intended; established industries elsewhere could complain of unfair competition with even more justification and demand similar privileges for their employees. Furthermore, it would defeat one of the chief apparent aims, namely, the preservation of the Africans' handicap of primitive tribalism for as long a period as possible, and violate what has recently become a basic tenet of *apartheid*. Yet if urban Africans are to lose their feeling of 'rootlessness', with a consequent mitigation of unrest, they must be allowed to acquire land and to live normally within an hour's journey of their place of work.

ATTEMPT AT CULTURAL ISOLATION?

The drastic attempt at geographical canalisation of industrial development into border areas – a facet of 'separate development' – is believed by some to be aimed at achieving more cultural isolation for the African than is believed possible in other urban areas and especially in the Western

---

[1] I am not suggesting that they had not felt deep resentments for many years.

Cape. Such an aim, weighed against the material sacrifice it must entail, might have some measure of justification if the mere avoidance of troublesome conditions could be accepted as a defensible ideal. But as E. C. Banfield has recently put it,[1] dealing generally with the underdeveloped peoples of the world, 'economic development, by hastening the decay of tradition and other forms of authority', tends to create ferment and disorder; whilst 'urbanisation, another indispensable condition of growth, also tends to produce political instability'. Thus, 'in India, Asia, Africa and Latin America the economically developed regions have been more prone to violence than the less developed ones'.

Such has been the dilemma of all rapidly progressive régimes. For instance, the enormous improvements in standards of living, health, security and equality of opportunity for the common people which were continuously engendered under the *laissez-faire* of the British industrial revolution produced unrest, discontent, occasional resort to strikes and violence, and opprobrium from superficial historians. Similarly the transition of urban employed Africans from tribalism must be expected to create trouble and unmerited criticism. But unrest and discontent do not mean disaster. The problems of adjustment – including those of the maintenance of public order – although formidable, are soluble. On the other hand, the attempt to isolate our Africans from the cultural heritage of the Western world does, I think, threaten ultimate disaster. It does so because it seeks to perpetuate injustice in the sense in which I am using that term.

The widely held conviction that the decision to direct African labour away from the Western Cape has been announced mainly for external propaganda purposes (in the hope that some means might yet be found for making at least some gesture towards its implementation without ruin) is not based on mere political bias. The critics do not believe that any government which actually tried to carry it out would survive a free election. It would mean that every farming constituency in the Western Cape would turn against the Government; for if urban Africans are to be

---

[1] *American Foreign Aid Doctrines*, pp. 14–17.

replaced by Coloureds, as is often suggested, these Coloureds would have to be attracted (or directed by future legislation) away from the farms; and if, at the same time, the farms are to lose their African labour they will face ruin.

CHAPTER 17

THE BANTUSTANS

DURING the gradual change of emphasis from 'baasskap' to 'separate development' in the interpretation of *apartheid*, the most important gesture has been towards the ultimate establishment of 'Bantustans'[1] – areas within which Africans are to be accorded a measure of political autonomy. The possibility of the reserves being treated as the Africans' national homes had for long been discussed, and the hope eventually emerged that, within these regions, it would be possible to claim that Africans had their own rights and privileges – political and economic – to compensate for what they lacked in the areas where most of them would continue to live and earn.

ORIGIN OF THE RESERVES

The origin of the reserves – the territories which, as the new Bantustans, have been promised more independence in local affairs – must be briefly sketched. Before 1913, Africans could legally retain or purchase land in the Cape and in Natal as freely as people of other races could, whereas in the two Afrikaner Republics there were legislative restraints on their land purchases. But in that year, the land laws of the four provinces were consolidated. The aim was partly to protect the interests of Africans by ending the continued encroachment of Whites on the already dwindling traditional African areas. Thus, in the so-called 'scheduled areas', Whites were henceforth denied the right to acquire land, but in all other regions – even in African urban locations – Africans were denied this right.[2] In 1936, the

---

[1] The term 'Bantustan' was, I think, originally used ironically. But through the official preference for the word 'Bantu' instead of 'African', it has come into general use.

[2] Unimportant exceptions to this assertion, introduced in 1937, under which urban land purchases by Africans could be authorised by explicit government permission, were abolished in 1963 under the Better Administration of Designated Areas Act.

restraints were strengthened. At the same time, however, provision was made (through the Native Land and Trust Act) for the gradual extension, by state land purchase from Whites, of the areas within which Africans could acquire land; but the actual expansion of such areas has been very small because of the high cost of land purchase from reluctant white farmers.

The first concrete step in the Bantustan direction was taken in 1959 through the Promotion of Bantu Self-Government Act. This Act established eight Bantu areas (the African 'reserves') within which there was to be co-operation between the Republic Government and the tribal authorities with a view to their eventual acquisition of local autonomy. Of the eight Bantustans originally envisaged, the only area to be offered this autonomy as yet has been the Transkei.

THE FIRST BANTUSTAN

The Transkeian Constitution Act, 1963, creates a Legislative Assembly of 109 members, namely, the four paramount chiefs, 60 other chiefs and 45 members elected by Transkeians living in the territory and by those registered as its citizens who happen to live outside.[1] In general terms, it confers a type of subordinate 'citizenship' upon every Xhosa-speaking African, unless he belongs to one of the other Bantustans, which might perhaps be established later. The 45 representatives (other than the chiefs) will be elected by all such citizens on the basis of 'one man, one vote'.[2] The

---

[1] There is a precedent for this in that Basuto Africans living outside Basutoland were permitted, in 1962, whilst resident (technically as foreigners) in the Republic to vote for their councils in the Protectorate. It should be explained that there had long been some measure of local self-government in the Transkei. The Transkeian Territories General Council (the Bunga) had functioned for many years, until, about five years ago, it was superseded by the 'Bantu authorities' system, which gave greater powers of control to the Department of Bantu Administration.

[2] The elections will take place under the shadow of 'Proclamation 400' which imposes a sort of martial law and forbids meetings of more than five persons without special permission. Moreover, the Minister of Justice has power to impose house arrest on, or detain *incommunicado* for 90 days, with no right of appeal to the Courts, any person suspected of endeavouring to further the ends of Communism or to encourage

Legislative Assembly will have the right (subject to the approval of the Minister of Bantu Administration) to tax all its Xhosa 'citizens', wherever they may be in the Republic.[1] Nevertheless, the Transkeian Africans (the Xhosa-speaking) will remain citizens of the Republic for external purposes and as such 'enjoy protection', although possessing no rights to vote in any constituency in which they may be resident or earning a living outside the Transkei. As a supposed *quid pro quo*, Whites are to be denied 'citizenship' rights within the Transkei.

All decisions of the Transkeian Legislative Assembly are to be subject to the approval of the Government of the Republic, and the Transkei will have no powers over defence, foreign affairs, immigration, railways, harbours and roads. Its courts will have jurisdiction over Africans only and not over Whites.

The emergence of this scheme was the result of a transformation of attitude which had come about very slowly. Nevertheless, it represented a remarkable change of front on the part of the party responsible, which had attained power through the promise of white domination – *apartheid* with baasskap. In 1950 Dr D. F. Malan, then Prime Minister and leader of the Nationalist Party, had reiterated categorically that they had always held 'that total territorial separation was impracticable ... Our whole economic structure is to a large extent based on non-white labour'. Total separation, he said, is 'not the policy of our Party and it is nowhere to be found in our official documents'.[2] Moreover, a few years earlier, the present Minister of Bantu Administration and Development had described the very policy for which he has recently obtained parliamentary sanction as 'dangerous if not more dangerous than integration'. He maintained further that any such ideas were rejected by the

---

violence. It will be all too easy to victimise effective critics; they will have no legal remedy as the law stands, and outspoken criticism of official policy may therefore be seriously discouraged.

[1] Unless the collection of these taxes is undertaken by the Government of the Republic, it seems likely to lead to widespread evasion. Moreover, the collection of the taxes may well engender all the friction and resentments aroused by poll taxes.

[2] *House of Assembly Debates*, April 1950.

Africans themselves. And only three years before the Transkei Act, Mr F. S. Steyn, MP, one of its chief defenders in 1963, described as 'crazy' anyone who thought that the Nationalist Party supported economic *apartheid*.

The 'Fagan Commission'[1] reported in 1948 that it would be quite impossible to bring about any measure of segregation such as is now intended. A few years later, the 'Tomlinson Commission', which the Nationalist Government appointed on coming to power in 1948 (to prepare a scheme which would permit the Africans to develop 'in their own areas', under tribal institutions and traditions) reported that the number of Africans who would have to find employment in white areas would inevitably increase rather than decrease in the years to come.

The Tomlinson Commission's two most important recommendations for improving the productivity of the African areas were ultimately rejected by the Government. The first was that private capital, under white direction, should be admitted freely to the Transkei and other African areas. The second was that the primitive system of land tenure should be abandoned and large-scale, mechanised farming techniques adopted.[2] These recommendations were, however, unacceptable to the Government on the ground that they conflicted with the basic objective of 'a social structure in keeping with the culture of the Natives'.

REASONS FOR 'VOLTE FACE'
The Transkei Constitution Act now inaugurates what *Die Burger* (the leading Afrikaans daily newspaper) has called 'a new period in our South African statecraft'. The aim is represented as total political separation and, as far as can possibly be achieved, total economic separation, with a conditional black baasskap (mastership) inside the Bantustans and an unconditional white baasskap outside them.

What has been the cause of this *volte face?* Some suggest that the pressure of world opinion at the United Nations and elsewhere, the clearly expressed anathema of Western civilisation generally, and the ominous development of Pan-

---
[1] The Native Laws Commission, 1948, U.G. 28/40.
[2] It is significant that the chairman of the Commission, Professor F. R. Tomlinson, was an agricultural economist.

African imperialism, have made it essential that some concrete steps, at least, should be taken which could be represented as examples of the benevolence of 'separate development'. Indeed, *apartheid* has had to be represented to the world, not as it had formerly been proclaimed to electorates, but as its complete opposite – an attempt to do justice to the Africans, as a means of responding to their legitimate aspirations.[1] The Government seems to have felt that it could hardly explain the ethical content of *apartheid* whilst still denying all political rights to the Africans, and that some advantages for the black people had to be demonstrable in order to justify the growing stringency in the administration of the laws to maintain order, and the laws which deny (outside the reserves) opportunities of advancement for the majority. Considerations of this kind appear to have led it to plan for a measure of local self-government – at present very restricted – within the chief African reserves. The intention seems to be (although pronouncements have been contradictory and vague) to allow these areas 'ultimately' to become sovereign independent states on a par with the Protectorates. But whether 'ultimately' is envisaged to mean one, five, ten or 100 years no-one yet knows.

A quite different view of the reasons for the revolution in approach is held by others. They regard it as a courageous and imaginative attempt to solve at least one of the great colour problems of the Republic. Political exigencies, they suggest, prevent the true purpose from being frankly and unequivocally explained, but the aim is to create circumstances in which Africans who are at present South African nationals will be seen to have achieved the same political status as the 800,000 to 1,000,000 foreign Africans at present employed in and resident in the Republic. It will then be possible to give complete political 'independence' and 'freedom' to Africans in their Bantustan homelands; and whilst their men (but probably not their women) will be free to continue to work in the Republic as long as their labour is required they will, on the Bantustans attaining 'independ-

---

[1] In appealing to the Afrikaner electorate, however, it seems to have remained expedient to emphasise that the object is 'baasskap'.

ence', have to renounce South African citizenship. Thereafter they will have no more right to find work or dwell in the Republic than Africans from the Protectorates, the Rhodesias, Portuguese East Africa, etc. They will then have no valid political grievances; for, it is argued, the areas intended for the projected Bantustans are at least as viable as the Basutoland and Bechuanaland Protectorates.

Whatever interpretation of the policy is accepted, it is obvious that it has been reluctant – forced on the Government because it rejects the thesis of the Progressive Party that the rights of minorities (such as those of the Whites in South Africa) can be effectively protected by constitutional entrenchments. It claims that nowhere in the world has a multi-racial parliament succeeded.[1] Yet this first Bantustan move has been rather a conscience-saving step, taken hastily without sufficient thought. Like most precipitate, ill-considered action, it may be expected to have all sorts of unpredicted and unwanted consequences.

HURRIED LEGISLATION

One would have expected a far-reaching piece of legislation like the Transkeian Constitution Act, involving great constitutional changes, to have been the product of long and mature consideration, with ample time allowed for public and parliamentary discussion and even eventual recourse to a referendum. In fact, it was rushed through the House.

In 1961, the present Prime Minister, forecasting the Bantustan policy,[2] admitted that it would be:

> 'a form of fragmentation which we would rather not have had if it were within our control to avoid it. . . . There can, however, be no doubt that it will have to be done with the passage of time'.[3]

Two years later, in 1963, action to implement the promised dismemberment had somehow come to be regarded as a matter of the utmost urgency. The immediate reason for the

---

[1] The contention is surely rash. Whatever defects may be alleged against the Mexican or Brazilian form of government, those defects do not seem to be a consequence of their multi-racial virtues.

[2] The Promotion of Bantu Self-Government Act of 1959 (see p. 152) was, in a sense, a forecast of policy; but the intentions have taken some sort of shape only in the Transkei Act.

[3] 10 April, 1961.

urgency appears to have been the necessity to put up a case in defence of South African policy on the South-West African issue. Thus, if the Republican Government could promise prospective treatment of similar generosity or enlightenment to Ovamboland as appears to have been accorded to the Transkei, there might be some chance that the International Court of Justice and the United Nations would judge *apartheid* less harshly.

The world has been told, partly through advertisements, that the African has been given 'the land his forebears settled', which is an area 'the size of England and Wales'. But not only have these advertisements given a quite false impression of the political powers transferred so far, but they have failed to make it clear that the Bantustan areas, about the 'size of England and Wales', make up only about 13 per cent of the area of the Republic; that only 28 per cent of the people of the remaining, so-called 'white' areas, of South Africa are white; and that two-thirds of the people (that is, about ten million Africans) are expected to regard the Bantustan areas as their 'homelands'! Even the Minister of Bantu Administration admitted that the provision of sufficient employment in the reserves to reverse the flow of Africans to the white cities cannot be expected to be achieved until 1978–80. But no realist expects, at the outside, that more than about one-third of the Africans will ever be actually resident in their 'homelands'. People do not choose to live in the territory for which they will have a vote but where they can earn their subsistence. And neither the Transkei nor the other projected 'homelands' can offer anything like the standards of subsistence to which the Africans have become accustomed. As the *Cape Times* has pertinently insisted:

'There is not a town or village in this country which is not more Black than White . . . the platteland is two-thirds Black . . . White South Africa on its own cannot mine an ounce of gold, produce a bale of wool or run a mile of railroad. . . . A real partition between White and Black of this country would leave the Whites in an enclave roughly equivalent to the Western Province of the Cape; and the gold mines, diamond mines and wool farms would not be in the White area'.

Much play has been made of the euphemism, the Africans' 'homelands'. But for the majority of Africans, the overpopulated and much eroded farming areas which make up the largest part of the Bantustans will never be more than their homelands of ancestry and affection, or to visit, never for residence. The homeland of Zionist-minded Jews everywhere may be in one sense Israel. But they expect political rights wherever they live because they are prepared to give their political allegiance to their country of adoption. Is it surprising that Africans should have similar feelings?

POVERTY OF THE BANTUSTANS

Moreover, not only are the Transkei and other projected Bantustans so poor in natural resources that they have, for some time, been declining in population; very little practical can be done, by means of any form of defensible state investment, to enhance their productivity. About half the area of the Africans' so-called 'homelands' is barren, semi-desert. Some portions are fertile and have a favourable rainfall, but the income per head was estimated by the Tomlinson Commission (in 1951) to be less than £13 per annum.[1] This income is approximately doubled by the export of labour, that is, through the income sent in or brought in from outside by the migrant Africans.[2] The same Commission estimated that the average income per family from remittances from Africans employed outside was nearly £19.

The poverty of the projected Bantustan areas has been aggravated because private, white-owned capital and direction has largely been excluded. Yet the Transkei Act still forbids all private investment from outside. This policy

---

[1] That is, rather more than half the present average for India as a whole, and about equal to the income per head in such primitive states as the Central African Republic, Niger, the Somali Republic, Chad and Upper Volta.

[2] These comparisons must not be considered as referring to the average income of Africans as a whole in the Republic of South Africa. The average African income is probably much higher in the Republic than the average income of Africans in any other country of the Continent. Moreover, comparisons of income of this type exaggerate differences; for the more or less self-sufficient poorer communities perform services for themselves which do not enter into national income figures, and for other reasons such comparisons may be highly misleading. See F. C. Benham, *Economic Aid to Under-developed Countries*, O.U.P., 1961, pp. 3-4.

alone will ensure that any industrial progress in the Bantustans will be reduced to a minimum. There is no doubt that the Nationalist Government has been shrewdly correct in recognising that, to permit free reign to the system of competitive capitalism, even in the poorly-endowed African areas, will be to allow a considerable rise in the material standards of the people and, in due course, far-reaching modifications of the tribal system.[1] Private profit-seeking would (i) prompt an immediate search for investment opportunities; (ii) stimulate as rapid an industrial and agricultural development of these areas as their meagre natural resources and their long distance from industrial materials and from markets would allow; (iii) result (on a small scale at first) in Africans undertaking not only skilled work but responsible and executive tasks; (iv) teach Africans how to promote business and industrial enterprises owned by themselves; and (v) lead to the demand for similar opportunities in the areas, outside the Bantustans, in which the larger part of the industrial employment of Africans will always occur. But it was this that the Tomlinson Commission's terms of reference had really instructed them to prevent by means of 'socio-economic planning'. As things are, any investment in these African 'homelands' from outside has to take place *via* the Bantu Investment Corporation, i.e., *via* the state; but the Corporation is responsible to the Minister for Bantu Administration who will be able to veto any developments which are politically unacceptable because they may seem likely to compete effectively with industries employing Whites.

The ostensible reason for excluding white-owned capital is the familiar one of protecting the workers against capitalist exploitation. 'We will not let the wolves in – those people who simply seek where they can make money in order to fill their own pocket', said the Minister of Bantu Administration.[2] Apparently supporting the common denunciations of colonialism, and condemning the system under which the Blacks provide labour and foreign powers collect the profits,

---

[1] See Chapter 9.
[2] 8 May, 1963.

the Minister contended that it would be wrong to allow the Transkeian people to be exploited like, say, the people of the Swaziland Protectorate. The Swazis, he alleged, were exploited by the British, who used that area as a milch cow and took away all the wealth.

Much publicity was given to the first Transkeian textile factory financed by the Bantu Investment Corporation. Few got the impression that it was a tiny concern with a capital of about £18,000 which is planned to begin with 20 African women employees and eventually to employ 60! If government policy were to divert huge sums of private capital, *via* taxation and the Bantu Investment Corporation, to industrial establishments in the Transkei instead of to the border areas, and if Africans there were to be trained for skilled work in large-scale, fully mechanised, assembly-line industries and remunerated at wage-rates sufficiently low to permit the sale of the full output, it might be possible to maintain intact the capital so transferred. But this is precisely what the Government and its spokesmen have been careful never to suggest.

GOVERNMENT PROPAGANDA *versus* REALITY

The South African Information Office has recently published statistics of the amount being spent for the benefit of Africans. It should have explained that the greater part refers to expenditures which have become essential outside the intended Bantustan areas. These expenditures have been thought expedient because most of the Africans are employed, and have to reside, outside 'their own areas', whilst the conditions under which they have been living in urban townships could easily shock the visitor from abroad.[1]

Again, in the advertisements in the overseas press the aim of the Bantustan policy has been stated to be that of permitting 'self-realisation to the utmost possible extent for each group. The Bantu of South Africa will work out their own

---

[1] The unsatisfactory conditions under which large numbers of urban-dwelling Africans have been housed (outside the mining compounds) until the recent change of policy arose mainly because they were prevented from entering the skilled occupations, even to serve their own communities, in the provision of conventionally necessary urban services. The restrictions to blame have been somewhat eased since 1951 in respect of the building industry. See Chapter 10, pp. 94–5.

destinies just like all other States in other parts of the world and Asia.' The world would naturally assume from this that complete sovereignty for the Bantustans is contemplated in the near future in an economically viable area. But most of the supporters of the Government have been left with the impression that real 'independence' cannot be expected for at least a century. In the course of the Second Reading debate on the Transkei measure, the Minister of Bantu Administration was quite explicit. He said: 'There will be no autonomy in the Transkei. . . . Where do you see it in the Bill?' The attainment of true autonomy, he suggested, would be 'a hundred year job'. And one of the Government's spokesmen reassured the House that 'the Transkei will have a long wait for independence, if it is ever attained at all'. If these assertions represent policy unfairly, the Government's own equivocation is responsible.

The Transkei scheme has to be seen in the setting of Nationalist ideologies. The constituencies which returned the Government to power have been continuously indoctrinated with the 'ideal' of white 'baasskap'; and their leaders have now had to explain that what has been termed 'self-government' or 'independence' in elucidations of the Transkei Act does not mean that there is or ever has really been any question of making the Transkei a separate state. 'It is', said the Deputy Minister of Bantu Administration, 'a means of maintaining white "baasskap" in white areas by allowing Africans "baasskap" in theirs'. But 'baasskap' implies the right to employ or exercise jurisdiction; and in fact no black person is to be allowed to employ a white person in the Bantustans, whilst Whites are not to be tried in African courts, but in courts falling under the jurisdiction of the Republic.[1] Moreover, in the areas of white 'baasskap', the Whites are never likely to exceed 30 per cent of the total population.

The Deputy Minister of Bantu Administration described the aim as that of bringing about the 'Bantu's self-realisation, materially and spiritually, within his own homelands'. The Xhosa-speaking Africans were being accorded 'full

---

[1] The Minister gave the assurance also that, as far as possible, no white witnesses would have to appear in Transkei courts.

rights' in their own territories because they were to be permitted only 'secondary rights' in the other areas (in which the majority of them have to reside in order to subsist). The phrase 'full rights' means, in the present Act, nothing more than certain rights of local government, in spite of many references to 'ultimate independence' in the debates and public utterances.

The Opposition tried in vain to obtain from the Minister of Bantu Administration a definition of 'self-government'.[1] He did assert unequivocally, however, that the Government of the Republic was sacrificing no part of its sovereignty. It seems therefore that there is no intention to create immediately, say, a Ghana, but rather something like a dependent colony (which is being done, incidentally, in an age in which the word 'colony' has become more or less a term of opprobrium).

One member of the Government Party contended that the Transkei would not be a state but would rather resemble a province in its status. Yet the State Information Office in London referred to it as the 'first Bantu State', and the Commissioner-General for the Transkei described it as a 'new self-governing State in its infancy' with the Republic as its 'Mother Government'. In effect, then, the world is told that the Africans are being led towards full autonomy, to be left absolutely free to govern themselves; whilst to its own supporters the Government adds 'subject to our agreement'.

POLITICAL CONFUSIONS

The inconsistencies in the pronouncements of Ministers at the Second Reading, as well as explanations by other members, were bewildering. But there seems to have been some directive from the caucus, between this stage and the Committee stage of the Bill, that Government speakers should be careful not to reject the idea of ultimate complete independence. Whatever assurances had to be given to the electorate, it may have been thought expedient that the record in the Parliamentary Debates should not be such as

---

[1] One Opposition member was moved to ask, ironically: 'What is it going to be, a non-self-governing self-governing State, or a self-governing non-self-governing State?'

could be quoted against South Africa before the International Court of Justice or at the United Nations.

The Government's difficulty in explaining the Bill apparently arose, then, out of its evident aim of satisfying both overseas opinion and the expectations of its own supporters. As an Opposition Senator complained, the electorate is being told: 'This is a minor measure and, under Government care, some small matters will be handed to the Transkei Government; important matters will remain under the control of the Republic'; whereas the world overseas is being told: 'This is a step under which the Bantu of the Transkei will enjoy independence'. On the other hand, the attempt by the Opposition to make political capital out of the Government's quandary led a member of the Nationalist Party to complain – not without justification – that:

> 'United Party criticism of the Transkei Bill depended on whom they wanted to impress. To the local white population they wanted to say that the Government was giving the Transkei complete independence and sovereignty. To South Africa's enemies overseas they wanted to say that the whole thing was a bluff and was only a smoke-screen for continued suppression.'

And some members of the United Party certainly did find it expedient to harp on the Black Peril, at least one complaining that the Government was 'doing everything for the Kaffir and nothing for the Whites'. At the same time the real aims of the measure may have been obscured by the Government spokesmen's attempt to avoid any impression of having been forced to give in to 'the Kaffir'.

But the most telling criticisms of the Bantustan plan, as it was disclosed in the Transkei Act, have given credit for what Dr Helen Suzman called its 'one encouraging aspect'. In spite of her having described the project as 'founded on fear and built on fraud', she said that it at least reflected:

> 'an awareness on the part of the Government that the political aspirations of the Africans could not be denied forever. This was indeed something, because it reflected a change of political thinking of the Government'.

The misgivings of the disinterested critics arise mainly because they have been left in no doubt about the reluctance with which the Bantustan era has been inaugurated, and partly for this reason, and partly owing to contradictory explanations, they genuinely cannot tell how far the benevolence of governmental utterances is matched by equally benevolent intentions.

The phrases used about self-government, whether intended sincerely or primarily for overseas audiences, may well prove embarrassing at some time in the future; for they seem likely to lead the chiefs to claim these words to record a solemn contract and to demand early 'sovereign independence' as it is understood elsewhere. Some defenders of the Transkei project have described it (rather ominously, I feel) as a means of achieving 'peaceful co-existence' with African nationalism which, they seem to imply, must inevitably develop there.

Professor P. V. Pistorius (an eminent political theorist who is a member of the executive of the Progressive Party), is one of those who regards the whole plan simply as 'window dressing'. He believes that it was never the intention to create an independent state in the Transkei but merely to limit its development to the agricultural sphere and to provide a birth place and a breeding ground for future labour in the white areas. But as I have said, other critics believe that the Government's aim *is* to grant complete independence to the Bantustans as soon as possible, thus placing all Africans in the same position as the enormous number of foreign Africans who find employment as migratory workers in the Republic.[1] When the removal of all African women from the Republic is complete – and present policy is tending in that direction – citizens of the Bantustans will have become alien visitors, permitted to enter the Republic only on such terms as the Government may enact.

OTHER ATTEMPTS TO ISOLATE AFRICANS

I should be the last to suggest that the Africans of the Transkei are ripe for representative government as ordinarily understood. Many are still very primitive in habits and outlook, and devoted to traditional tribal customs. But others, who may well be in the majority today, are at any rate striving for modernity and in process of fairly rapid

---
[1] See Chapter 10, 99-100, and pp. 155-6.

assimilation. An enquiry by the National Institute of Personnel Research discovered, in the study of one urban group, that 70 per cent regarded themselves as fully detribalised. And it is this partially assimilated group who are likely to create trouble, as the Government of the Republic realistically perceive. Indeed, the dominance of the chiefs in the new Transkeian Legislative Assembly seems to have as its constitutional purpose the concentration of influence into the hands of the relatively primitive. But if that has been the aim, it is likely to fail; for the appointment of chiefs is to be subject to the approval of the Department of Bantu Administration, and it is only too likely therefore that the chiefs will lose the respect in which they were traditionally held. They will come to be thought of merely as African representatives of the Whites.

Another apparent stratagem with the same purpose may perhaps prove more effective. An attempt was made in the first draft of the Transkei Constitution Bill to make Xhosa the sole official language. This could be an effective means of isolating the Africans from the modern world; but it met with so much opposition that after the introduction of the Bill it was amended to permit the use of Sethotho, Afrikaans or English. But there are at least five other Bantu languages used by the Africans, and when (if ever) the other Bantustans are created it may be necessary to give similar recognition to yet other languages. The prospective 'Tower of Babel chaos' (as the Leader of the Opposition put it) can well be imagined.

Yet the majority of educated Africans actually object to the use of the vernacular as a medium of education. They believe that the insistence upon Xhosa (or other African tongues) has been intended, first, to deny them fruitful contact with Western culture by preventing them from becoming articulate in the English language (for English is tending to become the lingua franca of that culture);[1]

---

[1] Some believe that the substitution of Afrikaans for English as the language of contact has been quietly brought about for the same reason since the Bantu Education Act of 1953, which transferred control of African education to the Department of Bantu Administration. There is unquestionable evidence of a rapid deterioration in the standard of English since 1953.

second, to preserve those tribal traditions which tend to perpetuate their backward condition; and third, to keep alive the ancient rivalries between the different tribes by preserving their separate languages on the principle of divide and rule.[1] If the Act is successful in ensuring that the Bantu languages remain the everyday means of communication of the Africans it will be just like excluding them, as Professor Pistorius has put it, 'from the benefits of science, of health and hygiene, and of the social and moral values on which we base our lives'. The wiser African leaders wish to rescue their people from their barbaric customs, ancient practices and superstitions, like faith in diviners and witch doctors, which are incompatible with the modern world. They see these traditions as impediments which the reading of English books and periodicals could be calculated rapidly to dissolve. Many of the attitudes which they deplore are responsible for the high death rates and particularly the high infant mortality rates in the African territories.[2] But the Government of the Republic still seem to be hoping that, through control of the Africans' minds, through careful determination of the content of their education, through the preservation of their languages, and through their exclusion from areas or spheres of employment where they compete with Whites, renewed vigour may be given to tribalism.

AFRICAN OPPOSITION TO TRANSKEI

The idea that the type of self-government offered to the Transkei is a response to the 'legitimate aspirations' of the Xhosa-speaking people would be difficult to substantiate. The Africans in that area did not openly press for any such

---

[1] One member of the Parliamentary Opposition charged the Government bluntly with aiming at keeping the various groups at one another's throats.

[2] It is true that the condition of Africans in these respects is better in the Republic of South Africa than elsewhere in the Continent of Africa; but their circumstances remain intolerable in a community which has advanced to the point at which a determined effort could eliminate the worst evils without unduly offending tribal sentiment. There is no area in the world in which it is more obvious that material advancement demands the abandonment of old faiths and revered traditions. But the better educated and more enlightened Africans do not revere the traditions of their people. On the contrary, they perceive that tribal influences, although sociological realities, are holding their people back.

move. At the only meetings in the Transkei at which the project was publicly discussed, clear opposition was expressed; and it was probably only the use of the Government's emergency powers to prohibit meetings (under Proclamation 400) which prevented more widespread and vocal protests.[1] Certainly Chief Kaiser Matanzima, and the Transkei Territorial Authority, of which he has been chairman, were consulted; they expressed the fullest approval of the measure; and the Government claims that they represent 95 per cent of their people. But they were appointed to office and not elected; and their unequivocal support for *apartheid* and their opposition to racial integration (which, they maintain, has been responsible for the racial disturbances in Kenya, Rhodesia and the United States) must make it obvious to all but the most naïve that they could never claim to be representative of the Xhosa people. They might claim to know better what is for the benefit of the people of the Transkei than the people themselves. Indeed, the measure of autonomy now accorded might turn out to be, directly and in its repercussions, the most important step yet achieved towards the attainment of economic justice for 'Transkeian citizens' in all parts of the Republic. Yet those who know the Transkei well believe that a referendum among the Xhosa-speaking Africans would have resulted in an overwhelming rejection of the plan (possibly foolishly, because it may have left them with more powers).

Bitter opposition has naturally been aroused among the small white population (about 16,000) who have been deprived of political rights in the Transkei. 'We shall be foreigners in the land of our birth', they have protested. They will, however, remain under the jurisdiction of the Parliament of the Republic and they have been assured, although in the vaguest terms, together with the Transkeian Coloureds (who number about 15,000), that their interests will be safeguarded.

---

[1] This proclamation prohibits meetings of more than five people without special permission. The Government claims that the last three years of martial law in the Transkei have been made necessary by white agitators, who have indeed been ingeniously active. It has been announced also that, at the request of the Africans themselves, the emergency powers will continue to be enforced by the Republic after the 'independence' of the Transkei has been achieved.

OPPOSITION'S CRITICISMS

The weight of parliamentary criticisms of the Transkei scheme was, as I have already suggested, weakened by the obvious intention of the parliamentary Opposition to make the maximum political capital out of any generous representation of the proposal. But the Opposition's warning that the move may lead to dangerous conflict cannot be lightly dismissed. For one thing, it will mean that an enormous proportion of the labour force in the white areas will be citizens of the Transkei (or of other Bantustans which may some day be created). One fear is that the new African authorities will demand the right to bargain with the Government of the Republic on the conditions of employment of Africans; for if free elections are permitted, the elected members of the Assembly are almost certain to promise spectacular improvements to their constituents. The Opposition are afraid – not unreasonably – that this will eventually create opportunities for Communists and Pan-Africanists to foster discontent and race hatreds.[1]

But if the new system of government does, in fact, confer on the Transkei authorities some real power to demand effectively the gradual dissolution of colour bars in the white areas – especially those imposed by labour union standard rates, minimum wage legislation and job reservation – the wise use of that power could of course benefit the Africans enormously. In other words, effective competition of the Africans with the Whites could be gradually brought about by successive mitigations of the barriers to equality of opportunity. But the present Government of the Republic would never respond to any such demands and they will, after all, retain ultimate political and military power.

It seems more likely that if the Transkeian authorities do exert pressure in this field, they will demand not better paid opportunities but higher wage-rates and costlier conditions of work for Africans in their existing employments. If they do so, they will be bolstering traditional *apartheid* and assisting the continued subordination and poverty of

---

[1] The Opposition have also drawn attention to the likelihood that pressures through the new African Legislative Assembly will result in the boundaries of the Transkei being extended at the expense of English-speaking farmers.

their people.¹ In industrial and commercial occupations such a policy could reverse more effectively than current *apartheid* measures an obvious tendency, in the absence of state intervention and controls, for Africans to command a growing proportion of the produce of industry and a more rapid increase in the real *per capita* wage-rate than that achieved by any other section of the population.²

Other critics of Bantustan proposals are apprehensive that the legislative machinery created will inspire the formation of an African fifth column. African nationalist demagogues are, it is feared, likely to be encouraged to exploit anti-white feeling. The danger is that black nationalist leaders will imitate the white Nationalist Party leaders of the Republic who have so successfully exploited colour prejudice and anti-British sentiment for political advantage. The inevitable ultimate necessity, under such circumstances, to use the Republic's police and armed services to maintain law and order within the area (and this is clearly a contemplated possibility under the Act) will, it is thought, be all too easily represented to the world as on a par with the Russian subjection of her colonial satellites in Europe.

These fears are not wholly without grounds. The Nationalist Government of the Republic are relying on the support of the chiefs and the survival of tribalism. But may they not be disappointed? In 1960, the British had expected (or at least hoped) that the newly established Basutoland National Council would reflect tribal conservatism. In fact, it seems to have become a medium of expression for the Pan-African imperialism with which African nationalism is allied. What some South African critics of the Transkeian project are dreading is that similar reactions may be ex-

---

[1] Any such action would be likely to produce a relatively small well-paid African force at the expense of the great mass who, seeking work outside the Transkei, will be forced to accept lower wage-rates on the farms and mines. Any policy which raised the cost of farm or mine labour would almost certainly be vetoed by the Republic.

[2] The statistics illustrate very clearly this tendency towards the relative improvement of the material standards of the Africans during the period which begins with the entrepreneurial evasions of the 'civilised labour policy' (under the stimulus of the increased dollar price of gold) in 1934 and ends with resort to 'economic planning' in the form of influx controls after the Second World War.

pected in the Transkei. In spite of the fact that Chief Matanzima and other Transkeian leaders publicly praise *apartheid* and attack both the white 'Liberals'[1] and the British, some shrewd South Africans fear that this is the purest casuistry. Matanzima has already claimed (without explicit contradiction) that the Republic's approval of Transkeian legislation will simply be 'a formality'; that he and his cabinet colleagues in the Transkeian Assembly will be free to select their own advisers in other countries; that he and his friends will be free to go abroad as they wish; and that they will be allowed to establish their own broadcasting station. The danger to South Africa is that, whether or not the Paramount Chief is sincere or casuistic in his expressed admiration for *apartheid*, it seems only too likely that powerful pressures – internal and external – will force him gradually to give way to the Pan-Africanists.

As the *Cape Argus* wisely warned:

'Outside the country the Government has described the new constitutions for the Transkei as "a major step towards sovereign independence". . . . The Government cannot state one thing to the South African electorate and another to the rest of the world; nor can it dictate or control the pace of the steps towards sovereign independence, once the first step, however faltering, is made. Chief Matanzima has made demands which can end only in a claim for sovereignty. When one leader makes such demands, it pays others to go further. There can be no reason to suppose that the Transkei will not follow the pattern.'

Moreover, the encouragement of the Xhosa people to direct their loyalty towards themselves alone, through giving them their own flag, national anthem and oath of allegiance is likely, many believe, to prove much less innocuous than the Government have imagined. But the Minister of Bantu Administration[2] dismissed a strong Opposition plea for the

---

[1] The South African Liberal Party is a slightly Leftist organisation which explicitly rejects Communism, advocates non-violence, but canvasses African support and presses for one-man one-vote in the Republic. It may have been used, however, as a refuge for Communist fellow travellers working for the cause of Pan-African imperialism.

[2] *Cape Times*, 2 April, 1963.

retention of a common citizenship with loyalty to one Fatherland.

APARTHEID NO LASTING SOLUTION

If the Government really are envisaging ultimate, true sovereign independence for the Bantustans, the move will, as we have seen, leave the Africans who had formerly been citizens of the Republic more or less in the same constitutional position as the many foreign migrant Africans from the protectorates, Portuguese East Africa and other African territories, who regularly find employment in the Republic.[1] But, said the Leader of the Opposition, in view of the Pan-African menace, a wise government would have welcomed every point of contact rather than have fostered the isolation of the Africans. Within a few years we may well see a disgruntled Transkeian Government appealing to the United Nations to intervene in the interests of Xhosa labourers who, by reason of the economic development of the African Continent, must find their subsistence in areas in which they are denied human rights.

White South Africa may be forced to pay a huge price for what many regard as the stubborn failure of its Government to face the problems of a multi-racial society. The concessions made to the Transkei have achieved nothing towards the solution of the problem of how political rights may be extended to the black majority (at present the 'have nots') outside the Bantustans whilst adequately safeguarding the rights of the white minority (at present the 'haves'). Nothing has been done to remove the increasingly resented stigma of blackness – the assumption that Africans are inferior not only by primitiveness of culture, poor education and lack of economically valuable skills, but by race and skin pigmentation. And nothing has been done to solve the problems of rights and opportunities for the Coloureds and the Indians, or the problems constituted by the indigenous races of South West Africa (in whose 'homeland' there were, indeed, no Whites at all a century ago).

The Minister of Bantu Administration had one very effective point in defending the Transkei plan. Neither the

---

[1]See Chapter 10, pp. 99–100, and p. 164.

Whites nor the Coloureds nor the Indians wanted integration, he said. Even the Africans did not want it. Hence the separation of the races was obviously the solution preferred by all. *But if that were true, there would be no need for drastic legislation to prevent integration.*

The Whites, the Coloureds and the Indians would, in the mass, like to be protected against the competition of Africans. And most of them would not wish to marry Africans. But I believe that all Africans would welcome the opportunity of competing more effectively with the privileged Whites or with the relatively privileged Coloureds or Indians, and that none of the non-white races would object to social integration with the Whites. I believe further (as I have already explained) that there is no genuine distaste, at least amongst the detribalised Africans, for intermarriage with races which enjoy higher social and economic status.

What is really valid in the Minister's claim is simply that all privileged groups and races would like the power of the state to be used on their behalf. They would all like to prevent profit-seeking incentives from dissolving the privileges and creating opportunities for the unprivileged classes and races. The virtue of the free market system is that it disciplines the inherent selfishness of man, makes possible an economic order which offers equality of opportunity, and creates thereby the conditions from which equality of consideration and respect are likely to emerge.

CHAPTER 18

THE MARKET IS COLOUR-BLIND

THROUGHOUT the description and analysis of South African developments the reader will have perceived the interaction of two sets of opposed forces, the first tending powerfully to liberate the non-white peoples of the world from inertias and coercions which would otherwise perpetuate historical inferiorities of occupation, training and status, the second tending to maintain or strengthen the coercions which hold the non-Whites in economic subjection.

The liberating force is released by what is variously called 'the free market system', 'the competitive system', 'the capitalist system' or 'the profit system'. When we buy a product in the free market, we do not ask: What was the colour of the person who made it? Nor do we ask about the sex, race, nationality, religion or political opinions of the producer. All we are interested in is whether it is good value for money. Hence it is in the interest of business men (who must try to produce at least cost in anticipation of demand) not only to seek out and employ the least privileged classes (excluded by custom or legislation from more remunerative employments) but actually to educate them for these opportunities by investing in them. I have tried to show that in South Africa it has been to the advantage of investors as a whole that all colours bars should be broken down; and that the managements of commercial and industrial firms (when they have not been intimidated by politicians wielding the planning powers of the state) have striven to find methods of providing more productive and better remunerated opportunities for the non-Whites.

UNLIMITED GOVERNMENT EXPLOITS THE POLITICALLY WEAK

The subjugating force is universally exerted through what we usually call, when writing dispassionately, the interventionist, collectivist, authoritarian or 'dirigiste' system or, when writing tendentiously, by euphemisms like 'the planned economy'. Unchecked state power (or the private use of coercive power tolerated by the state) tends, deliberately or unintendedly, patently or deviously, to repress minorities or politically weak groups. Thus the effective colour bars which have denied economic opportunities and condemned non-Whites to be 'hewers of wood and drawers of water' have all been created in response to demands for state intervention by most political parties (although in some of the most blatant cases, to pressures from those who have claimed to be 'syndicalists' or 'Marxists'). Of course, the extension of state control need not necessarily involve discrimination on the grounds of race, colour, caste or creed; yet in practice it does seem always to discriminate against the politically weak; and by reason of history, the non-Whites have (so far) usually fallen into this class.

Experience of coloured minorities in Britain today seems superficially to contradict the principle just stated. That is due to an illusion. It is true that, except through state tolerance of the occasional private use of coercive power by labour unions (in order to keep out non-white interlopers),[1] a deeply-rooted tradition of fair play has prevented conspicuous discrimination against the advantage of a small non-white political minority. But this is because the minority is at present so small that there is no political advantage to be won through the promise of legislative discrimination against it. What appears now as a powerful ethical convention hostile to racial discrimination will, I fear, prove precarious under the traditions of omnipotent representative government. Until the Courts are empowered to declare unconstitutional and void all laws or collective agreements which contain colour discriminations, open or disguised, minority rights will be insecure.

COMPETITION LIBERATES MINORITIES

The virtues of the free market do not depend upon the virtues of the men at the political top but on the dispersed powers of substitution exercised by men in their role as con-

---

[1] E.g., the exclusion of West Indians as bus drivers and conductors. Labour union efforts to prevent the employment of Italians or Poles in mining work should be mentioned.

sumers. In that role, a truly competitive market enables them to exert the energy which enforces the neutrality of business decision-making in respect of race, colour, creed, sex, class, accent, school, or income group. The reader will have noticed that at no time have I claimed that the free market which releases the 'liberating force' has been motivated by altruistic sentiment.

For omnipotent representative government (i.e., constitutionally unchecked government, without enforceable rules for making rules) to claim a similar neutrality, we would have to have absolute faith in the virtues of the men who hold, seek or wish to retain power, against the temptations to buy the support of majorities by discriminating against minorities. Virtue may triumph; but in the light of the realities of vote-catching pressures, it demands that the camel shall pass through the eye of a needle.

In a book published nearly 30 years ago, I argued that competition is essentially an equalitarian force.[1] In a country of racially homogeneous population, it tends, unless obstructed by sectionalist law and administration or the use of private coercive power (as by labour unions or business monopolies), to bring about the classless society. In a multiracial society, it tends, because of the consumers' colourblindness, to dissolve customs and prejudices which have been restricting the ability of the under-privileged to contribute to, and hence to share in, the common pool of output and income. This is because business decision-makers – 'entrepreneurs' – have an immensely powerful incentive to economise for the benefit of their customers, who collectively make up the public. Their success depends upon their acumen and skill in acquiring the resources needed for production at the least cost, and especially in discovering underutilised resources. Yet in some backward countries it is still

---

[1] *Economists and the Public*, 1936, pp. 81-2, 313-15, 319-23. The process of competition may be defined as the substitution, for the consumers' benefit, of the least-cost method of achieving any objective, which includes producing and selling any commodity. This is the most appropriate definition of competition, whatever the institutional arrangements which give rise to that substitution. A competitive system cannot exist unless the state performs its role; but under competitive capitalism the state acts wholly in the collective interest and never in the sectional interest.

regarded as a weakness that private industrialists should put their wealth 'into speculative and high profit-making enterprises, into manufacture of consumers' goods, rather than into basic industries'.[1] It is hardly surprising that the rate of economic development has most disappointed the hopes of rulers in countries where such opinions are influential. Labour is the most striking example of under-utilised resources which the economic interests of private profit-seekers would attract to more productive uses. Even in countries of homogeneous population, large classes of people will have been confined to work of avoidably low productivity and hence of low value as a result of custom reinforced by deliberate restrictions on competitive markets.

In a truly free enterprise society, however, it is the duty of the state not only to refrain from legislation which raises the income of favoured groups by making certain wanted things scarce, but to prevent private arrangements having the same effect by enforcing laws and procedures which are usually known as anti-monopoly or anti-trust. Indeed, the basic distinction between a competitive enterprise or free market system and a restrictionist system is that, under truly free enterprise, the contrivance of scarcity for the private or sectional interest is prohibited, whereas the only limit to the creation of scarcities by 'central planning' is the discontent which may be expressed through the ballot-box or, where free elections are suppressed, through the potential intrigues of groups manœuvring for control of the armed forces and exploiting popular discontent in the process.

In referring to 'truly free enterprise', I have obviously envisaged a form of society which the course of history has never allowed fully to emerge. In every country of the world, economic self-rule by the people is frustrated to some extent by state intervention to protect sectional interests. By 'economic self-rule by the people', I simply mean the democratic exercise of consumers' sovereignty. Under a free market system, income receivers as a whole control the economy through the discipline they exercise over decision-makers, through buying or refraining from buying the

---

[1] *The New India*, quoted in P. T. Bauer, *United States Aid and Indian Development*, p. 49.

services and commodities offered in the market. The present is a restrictionist, not an equalitarian or liberal age; and I know of no country in which the state forbids all creation of scarcity, that is, all action for the benefit of at least some politically powerful sections. There is, for instance, no country in the world in which anti-trust legislation, although widely and rightly applied to industrial and commercial activities, has been effectively applied to organised labour and organised agriculture.

In a free market system, however, in which the state has not been prevented (through the political power of sectional groups) from performing its co-ordinating role, the detailed pattern and rate of progress of economic development is set by responsible entrepreneurial planning. The form in which the community's resources are replaced or accumulated is then the result of responsible foresight and decision-making on the part of the business men who seek to avoid 'losses' and to make 'profits' in catering for the freely expressed preferences of the sovereign consumer.

STATE PLANNING PUTS SECTIONAL ABOVE SOCIAL INTERESTS

In a state-directed economy, on the other hand, planning in response to socially expressed (i.e., market expressed) needs is replaced by planning with political objectives. I have shown how, in South Africa, non-white labour has not been allowed to flow to where entrepreneurs have anticipated the highest yield from it; how for many years industrial managers have not been free to locate new industries or to develop existing businesses according to their judgment of prospective profitability; how socialist procedures have been increasingly devoted to controlling centrally the industries, occupations and areas in which the Whites, the Coloureds, the Indians and the Africans shall be allowed to work.

The ultimate motive for 'central planning' decisions is political – the exercise of state power for sectional interests – and the trouble about any system under which politically powerful groups are favoured is that the social interest is ignored. As Professor P. T. Bauer has remarked (of India today):

'The increasingly close governmental control of social and

economic life in recent years has tended to strengthen separatism by enhancing the prizes of political power and thus the intensity of the struggle for it, and for this reason it has accentuated concern with ethnic differences between the rulers and the ruled. . . .'[1]

When democratic precepts are honoured, political power confers no rights beyond that of determining non-discriminatory rules. Once the ability of political majorities to enrich themselves at the expense of political minorities is excluded by iron-clad constitutional entrenchments, all motives for central planning of the type which we have had in South Africa (for 'separate development') would disappear.

LIMITED GOVERNMENT THE ANSWER

Some argue that the defect of central planning in South Africa is simply that non-Whites are without effective political representation. If all races were properly represented, they believe, the power of the state could be used for the benefit of all, instead of for the benefit of the Whites. But this is a partial truth. Universal suffrage would merely mean the transfer of power to a new political majority, *with no constitutional limitations to prevent retaliatory abuse*. If there is to be a bloodless solution to South Africa's race problems it will, I suggest demand the acceptance of the philosophy of free enterprise, better described as 'liberalism' in its 19th century sense. The ethos of this philosophy is that it denies the right of the state to discriminate. Whilst many laws can be made only by majority decisions, the liberal insists that all the laws so determined must apply to all members of the community in the same sort of way. Under such a precept, as J. S. Mill acknowledged, the state may legitimately treat classes and races differently if, as a result of history, they happen to be primitive and uneducated. But the precept creates no justification for any *apartheid* ideal. Differentiation is justified only if it is being accompanied by genuine steps to remove the causes of the backwardness which has temporarily justified the differential treatment.

The truth is that parliamentary institutions (not only in South Africa, but in many other countries of the Western world) have been allowed to develop in a manner which

---
[1]Bauer, *op. cit.*, p. 7.

the great protagonists of democracy, J. S. Mill, von Humboldt and Tocqueville, would have deplored. Decisions by parliamentary majorities may conflict headlong with the democratic ideal unless the powers of parliament are rigidly limited and defined by powerful tradition or appropriate constitutional checks so as to exclude discriminatory laws. But the so-called democratic world accepted the form of government advocated by the apostles of a free parliamentary system without remembering or understanding the conditions necessary for it to function without injustice or tyranny. In any good society a ruling majority can be allowed no rights (a) to enrich itself at the expense of a minority or an unrepresented class or race; or (b) to attempt to maintain any historically determined status or privilege at the expense of a minority or the unrepresented. The rule of law must be a rule of non-discrimination and a rule, therefore, of limited state intervention in the sphere of markets and free contract.

The inspiration of racial discrimination in South Africa has not been solely the desire of the enfranchised Whites to hold back the economic advancement of non-Whites, or the hope of protecting the established expectations of Whites, or a determination to prevent the ultimate political supremacy of the Africans, which their rise in the economic and social scale seemed to threaten. Others thought, quite sincerely, that it would be a mistake to upset the peaceful economy of the tribal areas where the Africans were naïvely contented with their primitive ways of living, and that it was in the true interests of the rural Coloureds that they should remain as happy, loyal farm workers. But we have seen that industrialists and commercial men – for whose policies I have claimed no altruistic motivation – perceived that new and additional products could be brought within the reach of the community's income (hence causing that income to grow) if cheap labour, available through the recruitment and training of non-Whites, was used to the best advantage; that private business firms were always willing to invest in human capital, that is, in the development by training of the industrial capacity of Coloureds, Africans and Indians; that progress has often been obstructed because business managements have not wished to flout influential public opinion or the prejudices of their existing staff, or to fight quixotically against the 'political realities' of their time – the power of the state to make or destroy their fortunes; and finally that, whenever the more enterprising business men have seen some way of evading the legislative obstacles to non-white training and employment, they have done so to the benefit of the depressed groups and of the community.

In sharp contrast, the customs, prejudices and inertias which confine the non-Whites in the Republic of South Africa to low-paid work have been perpetuated by state laws and restrictions of organised labour exactly similar to the laws and restrictions that are applauded by people in all political parties who favour state direction. The survival of *apartheid* is, indeed, the survival of a kind of socialism – often altruistically motivated—whilst the dissolution of colour injustice has been continuously assisted by competitive capitalism. The persistence of colour injustice has been a triumph, perhaps temporary, for the ideologies of 'dirigisme'.

The age-old determination of white South Africans to continue to be both white and supreme can be observed today to be in process of transformation. The white intelligentsia are thinking more and more in terms of how to avoid black supremacy (a mere turning of the tables). For market forces, reinforced recently by a world opinion inflamed at reports (sometimes true and sometimes untrue) of colour injustices, are now making far-reaching political adjustments expedient. The Bantustan policy, so far enacted concretely in Transkei 'self-rule', has been a reluctant, improvised, clumsy move in the required direction. But it is only the first move. If a bloodless solution is to be found, subsequent moves will, I suggest, have to be framed in an understanding of the need for effectively entrenched rules for making rules – a constitutional check on the power of politicians who accept the responsibilities of government.

STATISTICAL APPENDIX

Population, Industrial Employment and Earnings in the Republic South Africa

POPULATION
(1960 Census)

	Total	Urban
Whites	3,088,492	2,581,731
Coloureds	1,509,258	1,031,063
Indians	477,125	397,101
Africans	10,907,789	3,471,233
	15,982,664	7,481,128

WHITE AND NON-WHITE EARNINGS IN PRIVATE INDUSTRY

Year	Average annual earnings per head		Average annual earnings per head of non-Whites as a percentage of earnings of Whites
	Whites £	Non-Whites £	%
1925–6	205	50	24.6
1938–9	232	56	23.9
1944–5	364	107	29.3
1946–7	406	117	28.8
1958–9	913	188	20.6
1959–60	957	202	21.1
1960–1	1,000	212	21.2

Employment and Average Wages In Private Industry

Number of Employees

	Whites	Africans	Asiatics & Coloureds
1946–7	157,016	251,125	80,851
1958–9	194,479	448,149	126,489
1959–60	193,835	429,120	137,721
1960–1	199,155	441,816	146,600

Average Salaries & Wages

	Whites £	Africans £	Asiatics & Coloureds £
1946–7	405.7	100.2	167.3
1958–9	913.1	164.3	259.1
1959–60	948.0	174.6	278.5
1960–1	999.1	184.8	294.8

SHORT BIBLIOGRAPHY

De Kiewiet, C. W., *A History of South Africa, Social and Economic*, O.U.P., 1950; *The Anatomy of South African Misery*, O.U.P., 1956.

Doxey, G. V., *The Industrial Colour Bar in South Africa*, O.U.P., 1961.

Economic Commission for Africa, *Economic and Social Consequences of Racial Discriminatory Practices*, United Nations, New York, 1963.

Fagan, H. A., *Co-existence in South Africa*, Juta, 1963.

Frankel, S. Herbert, *The Economic Impact on Under-developed Societies*, Blackwell, 1953.

Friedman, Milton, *Capitalism and Freedom*, University of Chicago Press, 1962.

Hutt, W. H., *The Theory of Collective Bargaining*, P. S. King, 1930; *Plan for Reconstruction*, Kegan Paul, Trench, Trubner, 1943.

MacCrone, I. D., *Race Attitudes in South Africa*, O.U.P., 1937.

Marais, J. S., *The Cape Coloured People*, Longmans, 1939.

Robertson, H. M., *South Africa, Economic and Political Aspects*, C.U.P., 1957.

Van der Horst, S., *Native Labour in South Africa*, O.U.P., 1942.

INDEX

ACT OF UNION 1910, 17, 19
African Mine Workers Union (N. Rhodesia), 108-9
African National Congress, 103
African, The, leisure preference of, 49-50, 51 (f.n.), 54, 90; 'tsotsi', 25; urbanisation of, 87-100; women, influx of from the reserves, 93
Afrikaans, 14-17; and English, 42-43
Afrikaners, *passim* colour attitudes of, 38-44; poverty among, 32-37
Aliens Control Act 1963, 100
Andrews, W. H., 60, 61, 68
Apartheid, passim
Apprenticeship Act 1922, 35-36, 74-75
Apprenticeship, Registrar of, 94 (f.n.)
Artisan classes, 35; emigrants, 58-59
Asiatic Land Tenure Act 1946, 124

BAASSKAP, 12, 110, 154, 161
Banfield, E. C., 149

Bantu Administration and Development, Minister of, 98, 113, 131-3, 137-8, 151-72
Bantu Investment Corporation, 159-60
Bantu Laws Amendment Bill, 104-5
'Bantu', reasons for use of term, 14
Bantustans, 95 (f.n.), 136, 139, 151-72, 180
Basutoland National Council, 169
Bauer, P. T., 176 (f.n.), 177-8
Benham, F. C., 158 (f.n.)
Board of Trade and Industries, 145-6
Boers, 15, 45-46
Boer War, 18, 50, 59
Border Areas, 95 (f.n.), 139-150
Botha, 61
Boydell, Dr. the Hon. T. H., 61 (f.n.)
Bristol-Myers Co., 138
Broederbond, 41-2

CALVINISTIC STUDENT UNIONS, Federation of, 44
Cape Argus, 100 (f.n.), 140 (f.n.), 170

Cape Colony, emergence
    of, 14-15, 137 (f.n.)
Cape Times, 20 (f.n.),
    119-20, 133, 140 (f.n.),
    144 (f.n.), 146, 157,
    170 (f.n.);
    and the controversy
    on the Constitution, 19-20
Chamberlain, Joseph, 45
'Civilised labour policy',
    68-81, 82;
    evasions of, 83-85
Colonialism, merits of, 11
'Colour Bar Act', see
    Mines and Works Acts
Colour discrimination,
    economic, 27-31
Coloured Affairs, Minister
    of, 20, 111
Coloureds, The, 14;
    as a privileged group,
    25, 26 (f.n.), 28, 73;
    building workers, 118;
    economic oppor-
    tunities of, 73;
    effect of Group
    Areas Act on, 111-2;
    farm labour of, 33-4 (f.n.);
    origins of, 15;
    political rights of, 18, 20;
    'skollies', 25
Communism, *passim*
Communist Party in South
    Africa, 60, 68, 126, 134
Compound system, 52-53

DE BEERS, 60

Defence Act, 113
De Mist, 15 (f.n.)
Diamond mining, 48
Die Burger, 154
Doxey, G. V., 28, 36, 63
    (f.n.), 92
Drift to the towns, 33
Dulles, F. R., 61 (f.n.)
Dutch East India
    Company, 14, 16;
    administrative system
    started by, 15 (f.n.)
Dutch Reformed Church,
    39, 40-42

ECONOMIC AND WAGE
    COMMISSION 1925, 79
'Eoan' group, 84

FACTORIES ACT 1918, 74;
    amendment of, 113
Fagan Commission 1948,
    154
Financial Mail, 143
Frankel, S. Herbert, 50
Free market, benefits of,
    173-80;
    forces, suppression of, 33
Friedman, Milton, 7, 15

GEYSER, A. S., 41 (f.n.)
Gold mining, era of, 47-57
Gold, price of, 50, 82, 139
Group Areas Act, 24,
    110-6, 124

HOTTENTOTS, 14, 15

IMMORALITY ACT, 24, 84, 113
Indians, The, 14, 121, 125; effect of Group Areas Act on, 110 (f.n.), 111, 124; immigration of, 17; success as traders of, 121-4
Industrial Conciliation Act 1924, 29, 36, 67, 74, 76-78, 94, 104; amendments to, 105-6, 117-20
Industrial Development Corporation, 141, 144 (f.n.)
Industrial Workers of the World, 60-61
'Influx control', 29, 73, 88, 93, 127-31, 141
Injustice, economic, 9-11
Intelligentsia, African, 26, 30; Afrikaner, 38-39
Inter-marriage, 11 (f.n.), 15, 25
International Socialist League, 60

JAMESON, 45 (f.n.)
Job reservation, 73, 85, 94, 117-20

KAUNDA, KENNETH, 63 (f.n.)
Knights of Labour, 59
Kruger régime, 45 (f.n.), 60, 112

LABOUR, MINISTER OF, 74-75, 103, 113, 117-8, 144 (f.n.)
Labour-Nationalist 'Pact', 69-70, 74, 85, 108, 119
Labour Party, South African, 69
Labour unions, formation of, 59
Langa Location, 90 (f.n.)
Liberalism, economic, 11, 173-80

MALAN, DR. D. F., 153
Mann, Tom, 61
Masters' and Servants' Acts, 102, 104, 106-9
Matanzima, Chief Kaiser, 167, 170
Migratory labour problem, 92-93, 99
Mill, J. S., 178, 179
Mine owners, attitude of, 53-54, 56, 64-65, 91-92
Mines and Works Acts, 62, 68, 69-70, 94, 119
Mines recruitment organisation, 54, 91
Molteno, Donald, 144 (f.n.)
Mozambique, attitude to colour of, 10-11

NATIONAL INSTITUTE OF PERSONNEL RESEARCH, 165
Nationalist Party, 18, 20, 40-42, 69, 110
Native Building Workers' Act, 95, 99 (f.n.)

Native Labour Regulation
  Act 1911, 102-3, 107
Native Labour (Settlement
  of Disputes) Act 1953,
  102-3
Native Land and Trust
  Act, 152
Native Laws Amendment
  Act 1952, 129, 136,
  139-40
Native Urban Areas Act
  1923, 128-9
Naudé, Rev. C. F. B., 41
  (f.n.)
'Ninety Days' Rule, The,
  134
Nkumbula, Harry, 63 (f.n.)

PAN AFRICAN CONGRESS,
  103, 134
Pass Laws, 29, 88, 126-7
Pistorius, P. V., 164, 166
Planning, central, 136,
  173-80
Poll tax, 33 (f.n.), 49, 54,
  126
Poor Whites problem,
  32-37, 58, 78, 85-86
Population Register Act,
  114
Poqo movement, 26 (f.n.),
  90, 147
Prejudice, colour, 11-12,
  24-31
Progressive Party, 144
  (f.n.), 156, 164

Prohibition of Mixed
  Marriages Act, 113-4
Promotion of Bantu Self-
  Government Act 1959,
  152

RATE FOR THE JOB, 72-73
Resentment, colour, 24-31
Reserves, native, 17, 21,
  47-57, 98;
  origins of, 151-2
Rhodes, Cecil, 45 (f.n.)
Rhodesian Federation,
  break-up of, 23
Robertson, H. M., 44
Roman-Dutch law,
  retention of, 39
Ruiterwag, 41
Rule of law, 11;
  abandonment of, 134

'SAY LAW', 34 (f.n.)
'Separate development'
  (*apartheid*), *passim*
Slavery, abolition of, 15,
  17;
  Chinese, 44, 45-46, 54-55;
  era of, 10
Slaves, importation of from
  Malaya, 15
Smith, Adam, 123
Smuts, J. C., 61
South African Act, see
  Act of Union
South African Industrial
  Federation, 68 (f.n.)
South African Information
  Office, 160-1, 162

Stallard Commission, 1921, 139
Status Act, 19
Steyn, F. S., 154
Suzman, Dr. Helen, 127 (f.n.), 163

THE TIMES, 135 (f.n.)
Tocqueville, 179
Tomlinson Commission, 1951, 91-92 (f.n.), 154, 158-9
Trade Union Council of South Africa, 104 (f.n.)
Transkei, 43;
  opposition to self-government of people of, 166-7;
  self-government, 22, 180
Tanskeian General Council, 19
Transkei Constitution Act 1963, 152-5
Transkei Territorial Authority, 167
Transkei Territories Civic Association, 137-8
Transvaal Miners Association (South African Mineworkers Union), 60
Transvaal Ordinance No. 17, 1907, 61
Tribal customs, preservation of, 11;
  ties of, 25, 88

Tucker, Josiah, 73

UNITED PARTY, 162-3, 168-9

VAN DER HORST, DR. S., 49 (f.n.), 90 (f.n.), 98 (f.n.), 140 (f.n.)
Van Riebeeck, Jan, 14
Van Selms, A., 41 (f.n.)
Von Humboldt, 179
Voortrekkers, 16-17
Voting rights of non-Whites, 18-20

WAGE ACT 1925, 29, 36, 67, 75, 80, 82, 103
Wage differentials, 71
Wage rates, 80;
  in the clothing industry, 143;
  in the mines, 55, 65, 72-73;
  in secondary industry, 97
Webb, S. and B., 72 (f.n.)
Wesley, John, 10
Westminster, Statute of, 6, 19
Wilson and Mafeje, 26 (f.n.), 111 (f.n.)
World Council of Churches, 40 (f.n.)

XHOSA LANGUAGE, 43, 88, 152-3, 165-6

LargePrintLiberty.com

Dedicated to offering books on libertarian thought and economics in Large Print paperback.

Titles include:

For a New Liberty, by Murray N. Rothbard (Philosophy)
"A classic that for over two decades has been hailed as the best general work on libertarianism available. Rothbard begins with a quick overview of its historical roots, and then goes on to define libertarianism as resting 'upon one single axiom: that no man or group of men shall aggress upon the person or property of anyone else.' He writes a withering critique of the chief violator of liberty: the State. Rothbard then provides penetrating libertarian solutions for many of today's most pressing problems, including poverty, war, threats to civil liberties, the education crisis, and more."

Principles of Economics, by Carl Menger (Economics)
"In the beginning, there was Menger. It was this book that reformulated, and really rescued, economic science. It kicked off the Marginalist Revolution, which corrected theoretical errors of the old classical school. These errors concerned value theory, and they had sown enough confusion to make the dangerous ideology of Marxism seem more plausible than it really was. Menger set out to elucidate the precise nature of economic value, and root economics firmly in the real-world actions of individual human beings."

Great Wars and Great Leaders, by Ralph Raico (History)
"In the backdrop of this blistering and deeply insightful and scholarly history is the whitewashing of 'great leaders' like Woodrow Wilson, Winston Churchill, FDR, Truman, Stalin, Trotsky, and other collectivists. They are highly regarded because they were on the 'right side' of the rise of the state. But do they deserve adulation? Raico says no: these great leaders were main agents in the decline of civilization in the 20th century, all of them anti-liberals who used their power to celebrate and enhance state power."